GEOFFREY CHAUCER

Geoffrey Chaucer was born in London in c.1343, the son of a wine-merchant. He fought in France, then went there and to Italy on diplomatic missions. Though he held various minor appointments at Court, he was often in debt.

His *Canterbury Tales,* begun in 1387, is one of the foundation stones of our literature and our language. His other work includes *The Book of the Duchess*, *The House of Fame*, *The Parliament of Fowls*, *The Legend of Good Women* and *Troilus and Criseyde*.

He died on 25 October 1400 and was buried in Westminster Abbey, in the area that became known as Poet's Corner. In the late fifteenth century, William Caxton selected *The Canterbury Tales* to be one of the first books printed in England.

MIKE POULTON

Mike Poulton began writing for the theatre in 1995. His first two adaptations were staged the following year by the Chichester Festival Theatre: *Uncle Vanya* with Derek Jacobi, and *Fortune's Fool* with Alan Bates, based on Turgenev's *Alien Bread*. Since then, productions have included *St Erkenwald* at the RSC, and adaptations of *Ghosts* at the Theatre Royal Plymouth, *The Dance of Death* and Euripides' *Ion* at the Mercury Theatre Colchester, all directed by David Hunt; as well as *The Three Sisters* at the Birmingham Repertory Theatre, directed by Bill Bryden, *Uncle Vanya* on Broadway with Derek Jacobi, Roger Rees and Laura Linney and *Don Carlos* at the Crucible, Sheffield, and in the West End, again with Derek Jacobi.

In 2001 his adaptation of the *York Mystery Plays*, directed by Gregory Doran, was performed for the first time in York Minster. In 2003 his *Fortune's Fool,* directed by Arthur Penn on Broadway, received a Tony Award nomination for Best Play, and went on to win seven major awards including the Tony for Best Actor for Alan Bates, and the Tony for Best Featured Actor for Frank Langella. Other commissions include two plays based on Mallory's *Morte D'Arthur* for the Royal Shakespeare Company, a new version of Schiller's *Mary Stuart* for Birmingham Repertory Theatre, and a dramatisation of *Gilgamesh*.

Other Titles in this Series

AFTER MRS ROCHESTER
Polly Teale
Based on the life and work
of Jean Rhys

ANIMAL FARM
Ian Wooldridge
Adapted from George Orwell

ANNA KARENINA
Helen Edmundson
Adapted from Leo Tolstoy

ARABIAN NIGHTS
Dominic Cooke

BEAUTY AND THE BEAST
Laurence Boswell

BRONTË
Polly Teale
Based on the life and work
of the Brontës

CINDERELLA
Stuart Paterson

CORAM BOY
Helen Edmundson
Adapted from Jamila Gavin

DR JEKYLL AND MR HYDE
David Edgar
Adapted from
Robert Louis Stevenson

EMMA
Martin Millar
& Doon MacKichan
Adapted from Jane Austen

GONE TO EARTH
Helen Edmundson
Adapted from Mary Webb

GREAT EXPECTATIONS
Nick Ormerod
& Declan Donnellan
Adapted from Charles Dickens

HANSEL AND GRETEL
Stuart Paterson

HIS DARK MATERIALS
Nicholas Wright
Adapted from Philip Pullman

JANE EYRE
Polly Teale
Adapted from
Charlotte Brontë

KES
Lawrence Till
Adapted from Barry Hines

MADAME BOVARY
Fay Weldon
Adapted from
Gustave Flaubert

THE MILL ON THE FLOSS
Helen Edmundson
Adapted from George Eliot

NORTHANGER ABBEY
Tim Luscombe
Adapted from Jane Austen

SLEEPING BEAUTY
Rufus Norris

SUNSET SONG
Alastair Cording
Adapted from
Lewis Grassic Gibbon

WAR AND PEACE
Helen Edmundson
Adapted from Leo Tolstoy

Geoffrey Chaucer

THE CANTERBURY TALES

an adaptation in two parts by

MIKE POULTON

NICK HERN BOOKS
London
www.nickhernbooks.co.uk

A Nick Hern Book

This stage adaptation of *The Canterbury Tales* first published in Great Britain as a paperback original in 2005 by Nick Hern Books Limited, 14 Larden Road, London W3 7ST in association with the Royal Shakespeare Company

Cover design by Andy Williams, RSC Graphics

Typeset by Country Setting, Kingsdown, Kent, CT14 8ES
Printed in Great Britain by Bookmarque, Croydon, Surrey

A CIP catalogue record for this book is available from the British Library

ISBN-13 978 1 85459 883 7
ISBN-10 1 85459 883 X

The Royal Shakespeare Company

The Royal Shakespeare Company is one of the world's best-known theatre ensembles, and aims to create outstanding theatre relevant to our times. The RSC is at the leading edge of classical theatre, with an international reputation for artistic excellence, accessibility and high quality live performance.

The RSC performs throughout the year at our home in Stratford-upon-Avon and that work is complemented by a presence in other areas of the UK. We play regularly in London and at an annual residency in Newcastle upon Tyne. In addition, our mobile auditorium tour plays in community centres, sports halls and schools in areas throughout the UK with little access to professional theatre.

While the UK is the home of our company, our audiences are global. We regularly play to theatregoers in other parts of Europe, across the United States, the Americas, Asia and Australasia and we are proud of our relationships with partnering organisations throughout the world.

The RSC is at heart an ensemble company. Actors, directors, dramatists and theatre practitioners all collaborate in the creation of the RSC's distinctive approach to theatre.

The Royal Shakespeare Company

The RSC was established in 1961. It is incorporated under Royal Charter and is a registered charity, number 212481.

A PARTNERSHIP WITH THE RSC

The RSC relies on the active involvement and the direct charitable support of our audience members for contributions towards our work. Members of our audience also assist by introducing us to companies, foundations and other organisations with which they have an involvement – and help us demonstrate that in return for either philanthropic or sponsorship support, we can deliver benefit to audiences, local communities, school groups and all those who are given enhanced access to our work through private sector support.

RSC PATRONS AND SHAKESPEARE'S CIRCLE

Personal contributions from RSC Patrons provide essential financial support for our artists, educationalists and their students, young writers and audience members that require special access services.

For more information, please telephone **01789 272283**

CORPORATE PARTNERSHIPS

The RSC has a global reputation, undertaking more international touring each year than any other UK arts organisation. Our profile is high; our core values of artistic excellence and outstanding performance can be aligned with commercial values and objectives.

Our extensive range of productions and outreach and education programmes help ensure that we identify the best opportunity to deliver your particular business objectives. A prestigious programme of corporate hospitality and membership packages is also available.

For more information, please telephone **01789 272283**

For detailed information about opportunities to support the work of the RSC, visit **www.rsc.org.uk/support**

This production of THE CANTERBURY TALES was first performed by the Royal Shakespeare Company in the Swan Theatre, Stratford-upon-Avon, in two parts. Part One was first performed on 16 November 2005 and Part Two on 23 November 2005

The original cast was as follows:

Nick Barber	The Squire
Claire Benedict	The Wife of Bath
Daon Broni	The Clerk
Dylan Charles	The Pardoner
Paola Dionisotti	The Prioress
Lisa Ellis	Alison/Constance/May
Christopher Godwin	The Reeve/The Physician
Mark Hadfield	Chaucer
Michael Hadley	The Man of Law/The Franklin
Anna Hewson	Emilee/Merchant's Wife/Dorigen
Edward Hughes	Nicholas/Aurelius
Michael Jibson	Absolon/John/Damyan/Crow
Michael Matus	The Monk/The Manciple
Barry McCarthy	The Host/The Nuns' Priest
Chu Omambala	King Alla/Walter/Arveragus
Ian Pirie	The Shipman
Joshua Richards	The Miller/The Summoner
Christopher Saul	The Knight/The Merchant
Katherine Tozer	Hippolyta/Maylin/Virginia/Grisilde
Darren Tunstall	The Cook/The Friar

All other parts played by members of the Company

Directed by	**Gregory Doran, Rebecca Gatward, Jonathan Munby**
Designed by	**Michael Vale**
Lighting designed by	**Wayne Dowdeswell**
Music composed by	**Adrian Lee**
Sound designed by	**Jeremy Dunn**
Movement by	**Michael Ashcroft**
Fights directed by	**Terry King**
Music Director	**Sylvia Hallett**
Assistant Directors	**Donnacadh O'Briain, William Oldroyd**
Company voice work by	**Jacquie Crago & Alison Bomber**
Casting Director	**Ginny Schiller**
Associate Costume Designer	**Emma Williams**
Associate Costume Supervisor	**Jemimah Tomlinson**
Production Manager	**Rebecca Watts**
Company Manager	**Pip Horobin**
Stage Manager	**Janet Gautrey**
Deputy Stage Managers	**Harry Teale, Alix Harvey-Thompson**
Assistant Stage Managers	**Olly Seviour, Jenny O'Connell**

Directors' Note

Chaucer describes 'well nine-and-twenty' pilgrims in a company that gathered at the Tabard Inn to set off to Canterbury that April morning. (Actually he can't count, because by my reckoning there are thirty, plus the Host of the Inn who joins them for the ride and Chaucer himself.)

The Host suggests that everyone should tell two tales on the road to Canterbury and two on the way back. It's a scheme which is never completed by Chaucer. They do not in fact reach Canterbury at all, and only Chaucer himself actually tells two tales, and his first is rejected by the Host as doggerel. The Knight interrupts the Monk's endless accounts of tragic falls from grace, and Chaucer just gives up on the Cook's Tale.

Some of the pilgrims tell no tales, and we've left them out: the Haberdasher, Carpenter, Webbe (Weaver), Dyer, and Tapycer (carpet or tapestry-maker), all members of a guild fraternity (on a sort of Trades Union outing), along with two more priests that apparently also accompany the Prioress, and the Parson's brother, the poor Plowman. The Knight's Yeoman doesn't tell a tale either, but we've kept him in! However, the Canon's Yeoman, not one of the original pilgrims, who gallops up at Boghtoun under Blee, a few miles outside Canterbury, tells yet another story, following the Second Nun's pious tale of St Cecily. And though Mike Poulton, our adapter and translator, gallantly represented both in his original text, and we went into rehearsal with both, we have cut them along the way. Who knows, they may reappear somewhere along our long journey. All the other pilgrims' tales are represented in longer or shorter forms within our production.

We have pretty much retained the generally accepted order of the tales, and so, as this book goes to print, the production should feature (among others), the Knight's, Miller's, Reeve's,

Prioress's and Nuns' Priest's tales in Part One; and (again, among others) the Pardoner's, Wife of Bath's, Clerk's, Merchant's and Franklin's in Part Two.

Gregory Doran
Rebecca Gatward
Jonathan Munby

A Note on the Text

This version of Chaucer's *Canterbury Tales* is designed to be spoken by actors and heard and enjoyed by audiences. To a reader unused to the unsettled spelling and pronunciation of fourteenth-century English, the early manuscripts of *The Canterbury Tales*, or Caxton's first printed edition of 1476 or 1477, or even a modern original spelling edition can seem like a foreign language. Or so we are led to believe. My view is that the spelling is a greater deterrent than either the vocabulary or the pronunciation and that spoken Chaucer is surprisingly accessible. However, I have modernised the spelling throughout and, on occasion misspelled words to indicate and make obvious how they should be pronounced in order to meet the requirements of the rhyme and rhythm of a line. For example, Chaucer's lines:

> And specially, from every shires ende
> Of Engelond, to Caunterbury they wende

I have written as:

> And specially from every shire's end
> Of Engerland – To Canterb'ry they wend.

When in doubt, the heavy rhyme should guide the reader to the appropriate pronunciation.

Where Chaucer's vocabulary becomes for today's reader dense and forbidding and would, in my judgement, threaten the understanding and therefore the enjoyment of the work, I have altered it. I have not modernised (though I have on one occasion used the word *wind-bag*, and confess that the earliest usage I can find of it is 1470) preferring to use alternative vocabulary that would have been familiar to Chaucer's own audience – except on a few occasions where, for the sake of a laugh, I couldn't help myself. Some words I've not updated because, though long out of use, they are familiar to us from other sources – such as Shakespeare. For example *wyght* or *wighte* (person); *whilom* or *whylom* (once upon a time); *certes* (certainly) are all well known. Other words I've kept because I love them, and because they are at the heart of the work, and help define Chaucer's greatness: for example *weymenting* (lamentation); *mawmentree* (the worship of idols); *wanhope* (despair); *fernë halwes* (far-off shrines); etc.

Most of the text is powered by lines of ten syllables familiar to us from Shakespeare's usual verse form. It's not always obvious where the stresses fall so, to help the actor and the reader, I have sometimes indicated what is required by accenting the syllable to be stressed (piercéd). I have not always done this. Sometimes Chaucer requires us to hit a consonant hard so that the last 'e' of a word almost becomes a separate syllable and indeed counts as one when calculating the ten stresses in a line. For example: 'And smallë fowlës maken melody' is not 'And small fowls maken melody,' nor is it 'And smaller fowlees maken melody' – a mangling I have sometimes, sadly, heard – but something between the two.

Another thing to note is the fluidity of the names of the characters in the tales. Chaucer often changes the form of the name in order to fit the rhyme and rhythm of the line. It is futile to try and standardise. For example, in *The Knight's Tale*, Arcita is usually pronounced Ar-kíte-a, but to fit the line he sometimes becomes Ar-kíte, and on one occasion Ár-kite. Emilee occasionally becomes E-míll-ya, and once E-mill-yá.

I have always worked from two excellent old editions of Chaucer – Skeat at school, and Robinson at university, both published by Oxford University Press, and steered clear of any updated versions, however excellent and tempting.

Mike Poulton

CHAUCER'S
THE CANTERBURY TALES

Adapted by Mike Poulton

Play One
Parts One and Two

Play Two
Parts Three and Four

For Greg Doran

'That never did but al gentilesse'

Characters

THE PILGRIMS

CHAUCER
KNIGHT
SQUIRE
YEOMAN (*non-speaking*)
PRIORESS
MONK
NUN
NUNS' PRIEST
TWO OTHER PRIESTS (*non-speaking*)
FRIAR
MERCHANT
CLERK OF OXENFORD
MAN OF LAW
FRANKLIN
HABERDASHER (*non-speaking*)
DYER (*non-speaking*)
TAPYCER (*non-speaking*)
CARPENTER (*non-speaking*)
COOK
SHIPMAN
PHYSICIAN
WIFE OF BATH
PARSON
PLOUGHMAN (*non-speaking*)
REEVE
MILLER
SUMMONER
PARDONER
MANCIPLE
CANON
CANON'S YEOMAN
HOST

CHARACTERS IN THE TALES

THESEUS
HIPPOLYTA
EMILEE
QUEEN 1
QUEEN 2
QUEEN 3
CREON (*non-speaking*)
CREON'S ARMY (*non-speaking*)
ARCITA
PALAMON
PEROTHEUS (*non-speaking*)
MERCURY
JAILER (*non-speaking*)
VENUS
DIANA
MARS
SATURN
A FURY (*non-speaking*)
200 KNIGHTS (*non-speaking*)

NICHOLAS
ALISON
CARPENTER
ROBIN (*non-speaking*)
MAID (*non-speaking*)
ABSOLON
NEIGHBOUR 1
NEIGHBOUR 2
CROWD

MASTER OF TRINITY (*non-speaking*)
ALEYN

JOHN
A HORSE (*non-speaking*)
SIMON, *a miller*
HIS WIFE
MAYLIN, *his daughter*

YOUNG SULTAN
SULTAN'S COUNSELLOR
OTHER COUNSELLORS (*non-speaking*)
THE POPE
CONSTANCE
THE ROMAN EMPEROR
THE EMPRESS
SULTAN'S MOTHER
3 SYRIAN LORDS (*non-speaking*)
THE WARDEN
DAME ERMINGILD (*non-speaking*)
A YOUNG KNIGHT
KING AELLA
FIRST NORTHUMBRIAN LORD
SECOND NORTHUMBRIAN LORD
NORTHUMBRIAN LADY
VOICE OF GOD
MESSENGER
DONAGILD, *the Queen Mother*
MAURICIUS (*non-speaking boy*)
ROMAN SENATOR
SOLDIERS, SERVANTS, LORDS, LADIES, SAILORS, *etc*. (*non-speaking*)

MERCHANT'S WIFE
DON JOHN, *a young monk*
PETER, *the merchant*
GUESTS (*non-speaking*)
SERVANTS (*non-speaking*)
A MASS PRIEST
PAGES (*non-speaking*)

JEWS, *as many as possible*
CHRISTIAN CHILDREN – *singers*
POOR WIDOW (*non-speaking*)
HER SON, *singer*
FRIEND OF HER SON, *singer*
SATAN
A JEWISH CUT-THROAT
PROVOST
PROVOST'S SOLDIERS (*non-speaking*)
ABBOT
BLESSED VIRGIN MARY
PRIESTS, CROWD, *etc*. (*non-speaking*)

ANOTHER POOR WIDOW
DAUGHTER 1
DAUGHTER 2
CHAUNTECLEER
PERTELOTE
7 HENS
COL-FOX
SERVANTS (*non-speaking*)
AGRICULTURAL LABOURERS (*non-speaking*)
MALKIN (*non-speaking*)

RIOTER 1
RIOTER 2
RIOTER 3
BOY
TAVERNER
OLD MAN
APOTHECARY
WINE MERCHANT (*non-speaking*)
OTHER TOWNSFOLK (*non-speaking*)

VIRGINIUS
VIRGINIA
APPIUS, *an unjust judge*
CLAUDIUS, *an informer*
SOLDIERS (*non-speaking*)
OFFICERS OF THE COURT (*non-speaking*)
SERVANTS (*non-speaking*)
FIRST ROMAN
SECOND ROMAN
ROMAN CROWD

YOUNG KNIGHT
PRETTY MAID (*non-speaking*)
KING ARTHUR (*non-speaking*)
QUEEN
8 LADIES
25 ELFIN LADIES (*non-speaking dancers*)
ANCIENT CRONE/ELF QUEEN
MARRIAGE PRIEST

SECOND SUMMONER
YEOMAN/DEVIL
CARTER
3 CART HORSES (*non-speaking*)
MABLE, *another old widow*

WALTER, *a young marquis*
FIRST LORD
SECOND LORD
OLD LORD
OTHER LORDS AND LADIES (*non-speaking*)
SERGEANT
MUSICIANS
MAIDEN 1
MAIDEN 2
GRISILDE
JANICULA, *her father*
A BISHOP (*non-speaking*)
EARL OF BOLOGNA
BRIDE, *16 years old* (*non-speaking*)
HER BROTHER, *12 years old* (*non-speaking*)
A PAGE
FIRST LADY

JANUARY, *an old knight*
PLACEBO, *his brother*
JUSTINIUS, *his brother*
WEDDING GUESTS (*non-speaking*)
PRIEST
SINGERS
DAMYAN, *a young squire*
A PAGE
MAY
MAY'S WAITING WOMEN (*non-speaking*)
PLUTO, *the Fairy King*

PROSERPINA, *the Fairy Queen*
ARVERAGUS
DORIGEN
FIRST LADY
SECOND LADY
DANCERS (*non-speaking*)
AURELIUS
BROTHER TO AURELIUS
SCHOLAR
YOUNG MAGICIAN
HUNTSMEN IN VISION (*non-speaking*)
KNIGHTS IN VISION (*non-speaking*)
DANCERS (*non-speaking*)
A SQUIRE (*non-speaking*)
A MAID (*non-speaking*)
MANCIPLE, *singer*
CHORUS, *singers*
A WHITE CROW, *singer*
APOLLO, *singer*
APOLLO'S WIFE, *singer*
HER LOVER, *singer*

HORSES, HOUNDS, TAPSTERS, SERVANTS, CORPSE-BEARERS, LORDS, LADIES, KNIGHTS, A LAPDOG

PLAY ONE

PART ONE

One: Prologue

CHAUCER.

When that April with his showrers sweetë
The drought of March hath piercéd to the root
And bathéd every vein in such licower –
Of which virtue engendréd is the flower –
When Zephirus eek with his sweetë breath
Inspiréd hath in every holt and heath
The tender crops – And the young Sun
Hath in the Ram his halfë-course yrun –
And smallë fowlës maken melody
That sleepen all the night with open eye
(So priketh 'em Nature in their courages)
Then longen folk to go on pilgrimages –

PILGRIMS *sing 'When the Nightingale' offstage.*

And palmers for to seeken strangë strands
To fernë halwes, kowth in sundry lands;
And specially from every shire's end
Of Engerland – To Canterb'ry they wend
The holy, blissful martyr for to seek
That them hath helpen when that they were sick

Befell that in that season on a day
In Southwark at The Tabard – as I lay
Ready to wenden on my pilgrimage
To Canterb'ry with full devout couráge –
At night was come into that hostelry
Well nine-and-twenty in a company
Of sundry folk, by áventure yfall
In fellowship . . . And pilgrims were they all
That tóward Canterb'ry would ride.

The PILGRIMS *burst in, led by the low-life.*

SONG.

When the nightingale is singing
The woods wax white and green
With leaf and with blossom springing
In April well I ween
And Love my poor heart is stinging
Pierced with his arrows keen
All the night my sighs go winging
In April well I ween.

The KNIGHT *and the* SQUIRE *come in leading the richer sort, and are greeted by the* HOST *and his* PEOPLE. *They sit down to dinner.*

CHAUCER.

A knight there was, and that a worthy man
That from the time that he at first began
To know the world, he worshipped chivalry –
Truth, and honour, freedom and courtesy.
He'd proved his worth in wars fought for his lord
Through Christendom and heathen lands abroad.
In mortal battles had he been – fifteen –
And championed our faith at Tramyssene.

With him there was his son, a brave young squire,
A lad in love with love, with youth on fire –
Singing he was, or whistling all the day –
As fresh and green as is the month of May.
Courteous he was – modest, and able –

HOST.

To board, sir! Supper time –

He hands him a drink, which CHAUCER *drains.*

CHAUCER.

And served his father when he came to table.
They brought no other servant but this yeoman –
An English archer – afraid of no man.
I rather like his silver Christopher –
You'd guess, by trade he is a forester,
And – here – we have a nun – a prioress –
An educated lady . . . more or less –

Most careful in her manners – sim'pring, coy –
And if she swears it's only –

SQUIRE *steps on her* LAPDOG *which yelps.*

PRIORESS.
By Saint Loy!

SQUIRE.
Oh, I'm so very sorry!

PRIORESS.
Oh mon p'tee chien! Poverino! Venez au maman! Pauvre p'tee! O la! La!

CHAUCER.
What French she's learned, in Convent-school inland,
In Paris they'd be pushed to understand.

MONK.
Let not my hounds see it, Lady. They'd bite its head off –

WIFE OF BATH.
Here – give it a bit of sausage –

PRIORESS.
Oh non, non, Madame! Its little stomach is tres, tres delicate. Vous comprenez?

CHAUCER.
Then there's a reeve, a miller and a cook –
A crowd of holy folk – and then, just look –
This woman here's a widow four times over –

WIFE OF BATH.
Five times, in truth. And who are you, sir?

CHAUCER.
O, I'm just – well – nobody – that is, nobody you'd know . . .

WIFE OF BATH.
Come sit by me, then. Come, sir will ye go?

CHAUCER.
As for the rest of this ebullient throng
I'll introduce them as we ride along –

HOST.
To board! To board! The meat will burn –

CHAUCER.
Great cheer made us our Host – good meats, wine strong –
And to our supper set us down anon –

HOST.
Lordings! –

CHAUCER.
Quoth he –

HOST.
You're going to Canterb'ry? Well God speed you –
And may the Blissful Martyr bless you too!
Now, I've a mind – as you ride on your way –
To make some mirth and sport. What d'you say?
I'd have each one among you tell a tale,
And he of us that tells the best of all,
Shall have a supper bought, at our expense
Here in this place when we return from thence,
For I intend to join you on this ride
To judge the tales, and also be your guide.
And whoso dares my judgement to withsay
Shall pay all we must spend along the way.
If you vouchsafe it shall be as I say,
Show me your hands – Come! Make no more delay!

The PILGRIMS *are for the most part befuddled, unsure, or unwilling.* CHAUCER, *who is drunk, speaks for them and is supported by the low-life who are drunker than he is.*

CHAUCER.
Well I say yes! Come on! Hands up! There's mine!

HOST.
We're all agreed? Good! Bring us then more wine!

CHAUCER (*singing*).
When the nightingale is singing
The woods wax white and green.

(*The other* DRUNKS *join in.*)

With leaf and with blossom springing
In April well I ween.

ALL.

And Love my poor heart is stinging

(CHAUCER *falls asleep.*)

Pierced with his arrows keen
All the night my sighs go winging
In April well I ween.

(CHAUCER *is left drunk at the table. Night descends. Cock-crow. Dawn. The respectable* PILGRIMS, *ready to set out, assemble and sing a morning hymn in honour of St Thomas.*)

HYMN.

Gaudeamus omnes in Domino,
diem festum celebrantes
sub honore beati Thomas Martyris:
de cujus passione gaudent Angeli,
et collaudant Filium Dei!
Exsultate justi, in Domino:
rectos decet collaudatio! Amen!

CHAUCER.

When the nightingale is . . . sing . . .

(*He wakes up, slightly hungover.*)

On the morrow, when day began to spring
Up rose our host and, crowing like a cock,
He gathered us together in a flock.

The HOST *does so. The* PILGRIMS *set out. Half of them sing 'Gaudeamus Omnes in Domino', the other half sing 'When the Nightingale'.*

Along the road t'wards Canterb'ry we pace
Until we reach St Thomas' watering place.

HOST.

Now let us see who shall the first tale tell –
He who refuses – he must pay for all –
So we'll draw straws. My Lady Prioress –
Draw first –

PRIORESS.
Moi? O no, sir – I'm sure to pluck the shortest.

DOG *yaps.*

Calme tu, p'tee! Calme tu!

HOST.
Come on, Come on! Pluck! Pluck!

WIFE OF BATH.
God send me a long one!

HOST.
Sir Clerk leave off your bashfulness
Why do ye look so glum and taciturn?
All – high and low – must take each one his turn.

MONK.
I – er – I wouldn't mind telling the first tale –
I could declaim in manner tragical
How some of high degree from heights did fall –

HOST.
No, sir, no. Just take the luck of the draw –

MONK.
Then . . . O give me a straw –

CHAUCER.
The outcome was the draw fell to the Knight
For which full blithe and glad was every wyght.
He said –

KNIGHT.
It falls to me to start the game –
I welcome this short straw in Jesu's name.

Applause.

Two: The Knight's Tale

KNIGHT.

Whilom, as olden stories tellen us
There was a Duke whose name was Theseus;

Enter THESEUS, HIPPOLYTA *and* EMILEE.

Of Athens was he lord and governour
And in his timë such a conqueror
That greater was there none under the sun.
Full many a mighty country had he won,
And with his statesmanship and chivalry
Subdued that famous realm of Feminee –
Upon a time t'was known as Scythia –
And wedded with their queen – Hippolyta –
And brought her home with him to his countree
With great rejoicing and solemnitee
And with her came her sister – Emilee.

Three WEEPING QUEENS, *dressed in mourning, throw themselves at* THESEUS' *feet.*

THESEUS.

What folk are ye, that at my home-coming
Perturb my celebration with your wailing?
Have ye so little feeling of our joy
That thus, in waymenting, ye shriek and cry?

FIRST QUEEN.

Great Lord, whom Fortune crowns with victory,
Long may you reign! Show us your clemency.
Have mercy on our woe and our distress!

SECOND QUEEN.

Some tear of pity, of thy gentilesse,
Upon us wretched women let thou fall –
For, certës, Lord, there's none among us all
That hath not been a duchess or a queen.

THIRD QUEEN.

Now we be beggars, as it well is seen –
Thankéd be Fortune her false turning wheel! –
For no man's state is sure – for good nor ill.

FIRST QUEEN.
I, wretched wyght, that weep and walen thus,
Was once the wife to King Cappaneus,
Slaughtered at Thebes – O curséd be that day! –
And these poor ladies in their black array,
Who make this piteous lamentacion,
All lost their husbands fighting for that town.

SECOND QUEEN.
And now that old fox, Creon, holds Thebes city
Who in his pride, and his iniquity,
For spite, for vengeance, and for tyranny,
Upon the bodies does great villainy
Of all our lords that in the siege lie slain.

THIRD QUEEN.
He will not let us bring them home again,
Nor will he suffer them by his assent
To be laid low in earth, or else be brent.

FIRST QUEEN.
But sets his hounds to eat them, out of spite.
O mighty Theseus, help us! Do us right!
And let our sorrows sink deep in thy heart.

KNIGHT.
This gentle Duke, then, when he heard them speak,
He thought for pity that his heart would break –
And swore his oath:

THESEUS.
As I am truest knight,
I'll bring down all my force of arms, my might
Upon the head of Creon, tyrant proud,
That all the Grecian folk shall cry aloud
How wicked kings will have their just reward.

KNIGHT.
What more's to tell?
Unfurled he his banners, and forth he rode
For Thebes, and with him all his mighty host.

A battle.

King Creon fought well but the day he lost
For Theseus slew him manly as a knight,
Pulled down Thebes' walls, and put her folk to flight.
And to the ladies he restored again
The bones of all their husbands that were slain.

A funeral procession.

The great clamour and all the waymenting
That the poor ladies made at the burning
Of the bodies – would take too long to tell
And keep me from the purpose of my tale.

Exit procession.

It chanced that on the battlefield they found,

ARCITA *and* PALAMON *lying as if dead.*

Thrust through with many a grievous, bloody wound,
Two young knights – handsome – lying side by side
The finest arms they had – richly arrayed –
Not quite alive, nor yet quite dead they were
But by their coats of arms and by their gear
The heralds knew their ancestry was good –
Princes of Thebes, cousins, of royal blood.

THESEUS.
To Athens with them.
Let them dwell in prison
Perpetually – I will accept no ransom.

KNIGHT.
And that was that – what needeth wordés moe?
For in a tower, in anguish and in woe
Arcita, and his cousin Palamon
Evermore are locked – no hope of freedom.
Time passeth, year by year and day by day
Until it chanced, upon a morn of May,
That Emilee, who fairer was by far
Than was the fairest, whitest lily flower,
Walked in the garden as the sun uprist
Among the curious bowers, and where she list
Gathering flowers, party white and red

To make a subtil garland for her head.
And as an angel heavenishly she sang:

EMILEE.
Of every kind of tree
Of every kind of tree
The blossom on the hawthorn
Is sweetest far to me
Of every kind of tree.
My true love he shall be
My true love he shall be
Beloved by every maiden
But loving only me.
My true love he shall be.

KNIGHT.
This Palamon, this woeful prisoner
As was his wont, by leave of his jailer
Was up and pacing in a chamber high
From whence into the garden he could spy.
Fate made him cast his eye on Emilya
And as he did, turned pale, and cried out:

PALAMON.
Ahhhh!

KNIGHT.
As though he had been piercéd through the heart.
And at that cry Arcita up he start
And saith:

ARCITA.
Fair cousin mine, what aileth thee?
To look so pale and deathly, what dy'e see?
Who made you cry? Who's done you injury?
For God's love, cousin, speak – O speak to me!
And yet I know full well . . . What could it be
More than our prison – our adversitee?
Some evil planet reigned when we were born;
We must endure. There's nothing to be done.

PALAMON.
It's not this prison maketh me to cry,

But I am hurt indeed, pierced through the eye
And through the heart.
'Twill be the death of me –
The fairness of that lady I can see –
There – in the garden roaming to and fro.
O she is cause of all my pain and woe!
Woman or goddess – how am I to know?

ARCITA.
O Lord what beauty! Now I'm dying too –
Unless I look upon her every day
I'm dead and gone. What more is there to say?

PALAMON.
Cousin, no more. I know you speak in jest.

ARCITA.
And if I do, may God grant me no rest.
I swear I love her – swear upon my honour –

PALAMON.
False, cousin, false! – What honour hath a traitor?
I saw her first – go ye and find some other –
Traitor to me – thy cousin and thy brother –
To love my lady whom I'll ne'er forsake
Nor never shall, until my heart-strings break.
Nay, base Arcite, thou shalt not love her so –
I loved her first, and told thee all my woe,
For which to me you're bounden as a knight
To help me in my love with all thy might.
Else ye be false – to knighthood and to me!

ARCITA.
Thou art a fool and falser far than I,
For fleshly love I loved her long ere thou.
What was it that thou sayst? Thou didst not know
If she were womankind or some goddéss?
Then all thy love is nought but holiness
As one might love the image of a saint.
My love is human, lusty, not so faint
And feeble sanctimonious like yours.
Then there's an end: 'All's fair in love and wars.'

KNIGHT.
They strive as did the hounds after the bone
Who fought all day then found the bone was gone.

PALAMON.
Love, if ye list, I love and ever shall –
I tell thee, faithless brother, that is all.
Each man is for himself, then – that's the law
While here, within this prison we endure.

KNIGHT.
On with our tale. It happened on a day,
To tell it you as shortly as I may,
A worthy Duke that highte Perotheus
That fellow was unto Duke Theseus
To Athens came, as he was wont to do,
For in this world he loveth no man so
As Theseus – and he loved him again.
So well they loved as all the old books sayn
That when Perotheus died – the truth to tell –
Duke Theseus went and fetched him back from hell.
Imagine that! And what is more he –

CHAUCER.
Let's get back, if you please, sir, to your story.

KNIGHT.
Now this Perotheus also loved Arcite –
He'd known him back in Thebes – and when his plight
Was told Perotheus, approached his friend
Who all at once decreed:

THESEUS.
Imprisonment hath an end.
You're free to go. But if you're ever found,
By day or night, in any of my lands,
With this, my sword, I shall cut off your head.
Now take your leave, and homeward get ye sped.

ARCITA.
Alas! Alas the day that I was born!
Now is my prison worser than biforn.
Now is my soul eternally to dwell,
Not in our former purgat'ry, but hell!

Alas the day I knew Perotheus
For then I'd ever dwell with Theseus! –
Though fettered in his prison evermoe
I had been still in bliss and not in woe,
Having the sight of Emilee the fair.
O Palamon, in prison maistow dure –
In prison? Nay, thou dwell'st in Paradise
That hast mine Emilee within thine eyes.
Thou art a knight – a worthy one and able –
That by some chance, since Fortune's changeable,
Thou mayst to thy desire in time attain.
But I that exiled am, and in such pain
Bereft of grace and fallen in despair,
That neither earth, nor water, air, nor fire –
Nor any creatures out of them that be –
May ease my woe, nor comfort bring to me.
Well might I die in wanhope and distress.
Farewell, my life, my lust, my happiness!

KNIGHT.
Upon the other hand, this Palamon,
When he was told that Arcita had gone,
Such sorrow made he that the prison tower
Resounded with his yowling and clamour.

PALAMON.
Alas!

KNIGHT.
Quoth he –

PALAMON.
Arcita, cousin mine,
Of all our strife, God knows, the fruit is thine!
Thou art in Thebes and free as is the air
And of my sufferings take'st thou little care.
Thou mayst, since thou hast strength and liberty,
Gather the young men of our family
And make a war so fierce on this citee
That by some feat of arms or forced treaty
May win my lady for thy wedded wife –
Upon which day I needs must lose my life.

KNIGHT.
Now lovers all I axe this question:
Who hath the worst? Arcite or Palamon?
The one may see his lady day by day
But in his prison must he dwell alway.
The other where him list may ride or go –
But see his lady shall he nevermoe.
Back home in Thebes, Arcite waxed lean and wan.
Melancholic he was – ever alone.
His eyes hollow – face grisly to behold,
His hue fallow, pale, and ashen cold.
Upon a night in sleep Arcita layed,
When Mercury appeared to him and sayed:

MERCURY.
Young man, to Athens shalt thou quickly wend.
For Destiny hath writ, thy pains shall end.

ARCITA.
And shall! Despite of capture, dread of death,
And with Emilya breathe my latest breath.

Takes up a mirror.

See how my face is changed and disfigyur'd
By all Love's maladies I have endured.
I might well, if I bear me very low,
Live by my lady evermore unknow.

KNIGHT.
He clad him as a povrë laborer
And all alone, save for his trusty squire,
To Athens is he gone the nextë way.
And to the Court gate went upon a day
Off'ring himself to drudge, and delve and draw
Whatever service men might use him for,
And found employment – sure 'twas Destinee –
With a Chamberlain who served his Emilee.
Short tale to make, he swynked so willinglee
That in a year or two his low degree
Was changed. Behold, in bliss lives this Arcite –
The much loved Page of Emilee the bright!
And told her that his name was Philostrate.

The whole Court held the youth at such high rate
They told the Duke that he should raise him higher –
Before he knows it, Arcite's Theseus' squire! –
Who gives him gold befitting his position.
Leave him in bliss. Palamon's still in prison.

PALAMON.
Look what I've done: this claret I have fixed.
Into it strong narcotics have I mixed,
Opiates rare and Theban potions fine.
Jailer, my friend – come – taste this glass of wine.

KNIGHT.
The jailer sleeps, the youth flees fast away.
The night is short, and at the break of day
Our Palamon must find a place to hide
So in this grove he chooses to abide
Until night falls. Thereafter he intends
To 'scape to Thebes and raise up all his friends,
And, making wars on Theseus, lose his life
Or win the fair Emilya to his wife.

The busy lark, the messenger of day
Saluteth in her song the morning grey
And fiery Phoebus riseth up so bright
That all the orient laugheth in the light.
And with his beams he dryeth from the trees
The silver drops that hang among the leaves.
Arcita wakes, looks on the merry day,
And for to do observance to sweet May
Out of the Court a mile or two he rides –
Draws near the grove wherein his cousin hides.

ARCITA.
May, with thy green, and all thy fragrant flowers,
Ease my sorrowing heart these wretched hours.
Alas the day that ever I was born! –
All is now brought to this confusion.
A Prince of Thebes I am – of blood royal –
Yet now I am so catyf and so thrall
That Theseus, Thebes' bitter enemy,
I must serve as his squire, disgracefully.

And what is worse, I do endure such shame
I dare no longer speak mine own true name.
No more a lord – No longer Prince Arcite –
Now I am Philostrate – not worth a mite.

KNIGHT.
Palamon hears this – and starts up from his thicket –

PALAMON.
Arcita! Traitor false! To me most wicked!
Now art thou caught that lov'st my lady so.
Thou art the cause of all my pain and woe –
And falsely hast thou duped Duke Theseus
To change thy name and thine appearance thus.
I must slay you – or else you must slay me –
Thou shalt no longer love my Emilee!
Now I alone must love her and namoe –
For I am Palamon! Thy mortal foe!

KNIGHT.
And straight away with swords both sharp and strong
They fight, one with the other, wondrous long,
So you might think this youth, brave Palamon,
Was in his wrath a raging wild leon
And as a cruel tiger this Arcite –
Like two wild boars they at each other smite –
Flecked with white foam, and sliding in the mud –
As ankle deep they wade in their own blood.

It's certain that in war, peace, hate, or love
All is ordained by powers that reign above.
So, for a while, let's leave them fighting thus
And come once more to treat of Theseus –
Who in his hunting takes such great delight
That it is all his joy and appetite.
And in especial all the month of May –
I tell you true – there never dawned the day
He was not dressed and ready for to ride
With horse, and hunt, and horn, and hounds beside.
And with him fair Hippolyta the queen
And eke Emilya, clothéd all in green.
And to the little grove their course they hold
In which there lay an hart, the huntsmen told.

PALAMON.
Thee I defy, that loves mine Emilee!

ARCITA.
Thou verray fool! Think well that love is free!

THESEUS.
Put up! Namore! Or he shall lose his head –
I swear by Mars that man's as good as dead –
That smiteth any stroke before me here!
Now speak at once, and say what men you are.

PALAMON.
We're dead men, Sire. What needeth wordés moe?
Fate hath reserved the death for both us two.
This is thy mortal foe – this is Arcite
Who once you freed, and banished from your sight
On pain of death. He came unto your gate
And told you that his name was Philostrate.
Thus have you been his dupe for many a year –
Did'st thou not make of him a trusted squire?
And this is he that loves mine Emilee –
For since the day has dawned that I must die
I may as well make my confession –
I was thy prisoner – I'm Palamon! –
That loveth so Emilya – fair and bright –
That I would die with pleasure in her sight.
But slay my cousin after I am gone –
Or slay him first, or else you do me wrong.

THESEUS.
Enough! This is a short conclusion –
From your own mouth, your own confession
Hath damned you both. And so prepare to die –
(*Drawing.*) I will not stay the fetching of a cord –

HIPPOLYTA *and* EMILEE.
Have mercy, Sire!

HIPPOLYTA.
Husband! Put up your sword!
Fie on the lord that does no mercy owe
Those who will kneel and true repentance show.

PALAMON *and* ARCITA *kneel.*

EMILEE.
Pity flows strongest in a gentle heart
And gentlemen that are of great estate
Should sooner drown their wrath in clemency.

THESEUS.
The God of Love! Ah! Benidicitee!
How mighty and how great a lord is he!
And in my time he made a slave of me.
And therefore since I too have felt Love's pain
And know how sore he can men's sense distrain
I will forgive them – Thank the gods above!
No greater fool than is a fool in love.
But here's the best of jokes – poor Emilee –
Raised such a passion of their jealousy
And knew as little of the hot affair
As doth, God knows, a cuckoo or a hare!

HIPPOLYTA.
To speak of royal blood and worthiness
Though that she were a queen or a princess
You both are equal to her royalty –
I speak now of my sister, Emilee –
But you must know she cannot wed you both
Be ye never so jealous, nor so wrothe.

THESEUS..
My will is this – so make of it the best –
That each of you shall go where'ere he list
And after fifty weeks – let's say a year –
Ye shall return, and with you bring me here
To Athens on th'appointed jousting day
An hundred armed knights ready for the fray.
And in the lists I shall make in this place
He that to whom Dame Fortune shows most grace
And from the lists away his foes doth drive
I shall give fair Emilya for to wyve.
This is my will and my conclusion.

KNIGHT.
Who looketh light of heart but Palamon?

Who springeth up for joy but this Arcite?
Who is most blithe but Emilee the bright?
The Princes kneel, and take their leave of all
Then ride home to Thebes with his ruined walls.

Three temples appear – or statues of VENUS, DIANA, *and* MARS – *each with an altar.*

A year hath passed, back cometh brave Arcite,
Palamon too – each with an hundred knights
And every one that loveth chivalree
To tourney for the hand of Emilee –
It is a lusty sightë for to see
In Athens such a goodly companee.
On Sunday night, ere day began to spring,
Young Palamon the morning lark heard sing,
And with a holy heart and high courágе
To Venus' temple gan his pilgrimáge.

PALAMON.
Fairest of fair, O Venus, goddess mine,
Daughter of Jove, mistress of love divine,
Take pity on my sorrows' bitter smart
Enfold my humble prayers in your heart.
Alas! I do not have the words to tell
The torments I have borne – I am in hell! –
And so confused I know not what to say –
My fearful heart to harm must me betray.
If thou hast mercy, Lady, on my pain
Then, surely, as my life these sides sustain,
I evermore thy servant true shall bee
And all my days wage war on chastitee.
Venus, this is my vow. Then stand by me! –
I'll fear no arms, nor ask for victoree
Tomorrow in the fight . . . Vain-glorious boasts
Of battle-honours plucked from vanquished hosts
Mean nothing to me. Grant me Emilee! –
To have, to hold, to wed, to bed – then see
Me die in paying her love's due.
How it be accomplish'd I leave to you.
Though Mars is strong in arms, stronger is Love –
Your vertue is so great in heaven above

That, if you list, Emilya I must wed.
If you refuse, then grant me this instead:
To have me spitted on Arcita's spear.
I cannot live to see him wed my dear.

He kisses the statue's feet, kneels, then throws incense on the altar. The statue shakes, then nods. Exit PALAMON *rejoicing.* EMILEE *enters and prays before the statue of* DIANA.

EMILEE.
Chaste goddess of the groves and woodlands green,
Virgin Diana, that my heart hast seen,
And know'st, before I speak, what I would say:
I long to live a maiden all my days
And be forever in thy company –
For I love hunting, and all venereye –
To tread the moorlands and the forest wild.
I would not be a wife, nor get a child,
Nor grant my maidenhood to any man.
Now help me, Lady, since I know ye can,
Send love and peace betwixt my suitors twain.
Shield their hot lust and turn it back again
That all their burning torments, and their fire
Be cooled and quenched, or else their hot desire
Spent not on me, but in some other place.
If it befall ye do me not this grace,
Or if my destinee decrees it so
That I perforce must have one of those two,
Then grant me him that most desireth me.
Though my own choosing is for chastitee.

Blood bubbles up from the fresh green twigs on DIANA*'s altar and the fire is extinguished in steam and groans.* EMILEE *is 'sore aghast' and weeps.*

DIANA.
Beloved daughter, know it may not be.
The gods in council high have it affirmed
In words eternal and by fate confirmed
Thou shalt be wedded unto one of two
Who so much blood and tears have spent for you.

But which of them it is shall thee possess
I may not tell. Come – end here your distress.

EMILEE.
I bow my knee, obeying fate's commands
And place my heart, Diana, in thy hands.

DIANA *disappears*. EMILEE *exits*. ARCITA *enters to pray before the statue of* MARS.

ARCITA.
Mightiest of gods, O sovereign lord of war!
Give me the victory – I ask namore.
I lay my youth, my strength, my life before ye.
Mine be the labour, but thine the glory!

MARS *smiles, the doors shake, thunder and lightning, the fires on* MARS' *altar blaze brightly,* ARCITA *makes a sacrifice on the altar.*

MARS (*in a voice as if from afar off*).
Victory! Victory! Victory!

KNIGHT.
The great day's come – it's not yet fully prime –
The people in their places in good time
And Theseus enthronéd rich and high,
Hippolyta the queen, and Emilee,
And other ladies glittering like stars –
In through the western gate – the gate of Mars –
Comes bold Arcita with his hundred knights,
Their banners red as blood – as, all in white,
From eastward enters lusty Palamon
At Venus' gate amid a host – so strong
That none might say who hath the avauntáge
In high estate, in worthiness, or age.
The gates are shut and Theseus cries aloud:

THESEUS.
Now do your devoir, all ye young knights proud!

Trumpets sound, a noisy battle.

KNIGHT.
Now shiv'ren shafts upon the shieldës thick!

Now some doth feel through heartës' bone the prick!
Up springen spears full twenty foot in height –
Out go the swords that flash like silver bright
Helmets to hew and armour all to-shred.
Out spurts the blood, like rivers running red.
With mighty maces broke is many a bone –
The hurtling horse goes down – his rider thrown.

But Palamon, as he hacks at Arcite,
Making his sword deep in his flesh to bite,
Some twenty knights by force the brave youth take
And drag him, still unyielding, to the stake.
Palamon's lost the fight. Arcita's won.
Theseus, when he sees, cries:

THESEUS.
Ho! It's done!
I am true judge, what I decide shall be:
Then young Arcita shall have Emilee,
That by his fortune hath the fair maid gained.

KNIGHT.
And Venus, up in heav'n cries:

VENUS.
I am shamed! –

ARCITA, *on horseback, parades around the tilt-yard to receive the applause of the crowd, and especially of* EMILEE.

KNIGHT.
Weeps her defeat – her tears will never cease
'Til Saturn speaks:

SATURN.
Fair daughter, hold thy peace.
Mars hath his will – his knight hath had his boon –
But – this I swear – ye shall have your way soon.

KNIGHT.
Look on the victor: Joy is in his heart.
Out of the ground, unseen, a Fury starts,
Sent by King Pluto, god and lord of hell,
On Saturn's orders – he's in the plot as well –

At which Arcita's horse, doth leap and skip.
Afore the proud young man can get a grip
He's pitched over the pommel, on his head,
And stretched out on the ground like one that's dead,
His rib-cage crushed upon his saddle bow,
Black in the face as raven, coal, or crow.
He's carried home by all his companee
And always crying out for:

ARCITA.
Emilee! Emilee! Emilee!

KNIGHT.
Duke Theseus then, with all his companee
Is comen home to Athens – his citee –
All full of joy, with great solemnitee.

All be it this misfortune came about, he
Thought it bad form to let it spoil the party.
Besides, men sayed Arcita would not die –
Doctors would heal him of his maladeye.
What did they know? When doctors do their work . . .
Physick farewell! Go bear the corpse to church.

PALAMON, EMILEE, THESEUS, HIPPOLYTA *and others in black at* ARCITA*'s deathbed.*

ARCITA.
Alas, for woe! Alas, the pain's too strong
That I for you have suffered, and too long.
Alas, my death! Alas, mine Emilee!
Fate hath decreed I'm barred your companee!
Queen of my heart – Alas, my almost wife –
Life of all love, love's centre all my life! –
What is this world? What – when the tale is told? –
Now I'm in love – now laid in earth, stone cold.
Cold and alone – graves shun societee –
Farewell my love, my sweetest enemee!
Now – hold me gently – in your arms me lay –
And – for God's love – take heed to what I say:
In all this world I know no better man
Worthy to have your love than Palamon . . .
Have mercy . . . Emilee . . .

KNIGHT.
His spirit leaves – some otherwhere to dwell
Where that might be I, and no man, can tell –
I never went upon that pilgrimáge.

Weeping and wailing, as ARCITA *is placed on an enormous funeral pyre.*

Forests are felled to make the funeral fire.
To name the trees were thrown upon the pyre –
As oak, fir, birch, hawthórn, ash, box, and laurel,
Beech, yew, plane, elm, maple and hazel –
I will not try, nor speak of it namore.
I'll leave it out – the preparation – Nor
Tell how woodland gods run up and down
Disherited of habitacioún
Where they were wont to rest and take their ease –
Nymphs, Satyrs, Faunes, and Hamedreyëdés –
Nor how the beasts, and all the birdës small
Fledden in fear, as down those great trees fall.
Nor how poor Emilee, as was the way,
Kindled the flames, upon the funeral day,
Nor how Arcite was burned to ashes cold
Nor of the great lyke-wake was for him hold.
But straightway to the point now will I wend
And maken of mine tragedy, an end.

THESEUS.
All things must end; As gods who reign above
Have bound all things in one great chain of love –
The fire, the air, the fruitful earth, the sea
Are set in bonds from which they may not flee.
Each thing that lives – each man and nation –
The gods grant time – a short duration –
A little dream – a little, little space,
Beyond which limits they may never pace.
Behold, the oak – how long its nourishing
When from the acorn first that tree doth spring
Living, it seems, forever strong and tall.
But in the end the mightiest oak must fall.
The very stones we tread on day by day,

Though we perceive it not, are worn away.
And out of this, we see all men must die,
Low-born and dukes – we wend all the same way.
Then is it wisdom – so it seems to me –
To maken virtue of necessitee,
And take it well that we may not eschew –
I mean that death to all of us is due.
What good can come of this confusión?
Have patience, friends. Hear my conclusion.
Let's thank the gods for all their gifts of grace
And ere that we departen from this place
I counsel that we make of sorrows two
One perfect joy to last for evermoe.
Sister. See – Palamon that gentle knight
That loveth you with will, and heart, and might,
And hath done alway since he first you saw.
Here take him for your lord – I say namore.
He comes of kings, but even were he poor,
Since he hath been your servant all his life,
Here stands a husband – if y'll be his wife.

KNIGHT.
And so with bliss, with mirth, and melody
This Palamon hath wed his Emilee.
And God that all the wondrous world hath wrought
Send him all love, that hath it dearly bought.
Thus endeth Palamon and Emilee
And God save all this gentle companee.

ALL.
Amen!

General cheers, applause, and congratulations from the better sort.

MONK.
A noble story –

PRIORESS.
I like a tale of love –

SQUIRE.
Or one of glory –

HOST.
Well done! We're on our way! The game's begun –
Now let me see – who'll tell another one? –

MONK.
I will.

HOST.
Well then, Sir Monk, let's have it if ye can –

WIFE OF BATH.
I swear, Sir Monk, you've got a lovely skin
Oh what a manly man! Now curse those kin
Of yours – God give 'em all confusion –
That put thee to a life of religion!
Thou would'st have been a cock to tread a hen
Hadd'stow been free to do thy will with 'em –
Thou would's have gotten many a lusty lad –

CHAUCER.
This Monk's a good fellow – a manly man
And fit to be an abbot or a prior
He's not a man to waste time in the choir –
He loves his horses, greyhounds and the chase
And follows after all things new apace.
The ancient rule – Saint Maur's and Saint Benait –
Because they are so strict and out of date –
He sets aside – 'not worth a pluckëd hen!
Who saith that hunters can't be holy men?'
And I say his opinion is good –

HOST.
Come, sir.

MONK.
I will bewail in manner tragical
How some of high degree from heights did fall –

CHAUCER.
Yes, I say his opinion is right –
Why should a monk be reading day and night
Scripture and Holy writ, shut in his cell –
And then Saint Austin bids monks *work* as well! –
To labour with their hands, to swink and sweat –

MONK.
I will bewail –

CHAUCER.
To swink and sweat! Why shouldn't monks have fun?
Let Austin stick his swinking up –

MONK.
I will bewail –

MILLER (*over the* MONK).
What's going on? –

HOST.
Robin, abide. You've drunk too much good ale.

MILLER.
I've got a jest to cap the good knight's tale –

HOST.
No, Robin, no! Not yet my levë brother –
A better man shall tell us first another.

MILLER.
What better man? Now harken what I say –

HOST.
No! –

MILLER.
If I can't tell my tale I'll go my way.

HOST.
The devil take you then! Your wits are gone –
Peace now, ye fool, your brains are overflown
With drink. Proceed, sir Monk –

MONK.
I will bewail –

MILLER.
I do protest I'm drunk –
S'if I misspeke, or wander in my tale,
I prithee, put the blame on Southwark Ale,
For I will tell the legend and the life
Both of a carpenter, and of his wife,
And how a clerk of Oxford set his cap –

REEVE.
Ho! Stint thy clapp!
Let be thy lewd, and drunken harlotree!
It is a sin, a foolish sin, perdee! –
To slander any man or him defame,
Or cast upon his wife such tales of shame –

CHAUCER.
This is the reeve, a cunning, choleric man
Grown rich by filching anything he can.
His Lord's not twenty – innocent – a child
In money matters easily beguiled.
D'you like his horse? The grey – a right good stot –
A stallion you would say – his name is Scot.

MILLER.
My levë brother, by my life I swear
That just because you are a carpenter –
And have a wife – I aim no jests at you.
Now many men have wives – I have one too –
She doesn't make me cuckold – never doubt it! –
If yours does you, I've never heard about it.

REEVE.
Churl!

CHAUCER.
A warning, friends. I fear the tale he'll tell
Will show us harlotry – bare flesh as well.
A shame, I say! That things begun i'th'height

Nods to the KNIGHT.

Should sink so low so soon – just to delight
The smutty-minded – those of simple wit.
I say, good folk, let's stand no more of it:
Those who are for high morals and good taste
Should now be gone. Depart. Away. Make haste . . .

Three: The Miller's Tale

MILLER.

Whylom there dwelt a man in Oxenford,
Old, dry, and rich, who took in guests to board
But of his craft he was a carpenter
And in his house there dwelt a poor scholar
Who studied hard. Such was his fantasee
He set himself to learn astrologee
And told men's fortunes – what should them betide –
Earning good money at it on the side.
He kept his chamber fragrant, clean and neat
With quinces, spice, and fresh plucked herbës sweet,
But sweeter far was this young lad, I says,
More like a maiden in his looks and ways.
As gentle Nicholas the youth was known . . .
How he relieved his lust when on his own
I dare not tell – he kept his door shut tight –
Spending his private time in self-delight.
This carpenter had wedded new a wife
Which that he lovéd more than all his life
And years of age she was barely eighteen
Jealous he was, and kept a tightë rein,
For she was wild and young, and he was old,
And greatly feared that he should be cuckold
She was a primrose waiting to be plucked –
A piggy's eye! – Just asking –

PRIORESS.

Oh!

REEVE.

What did I tell ye?

MILLER.

What was it I said? –
Fit for a lord to leg her in his bed.
There comes a time – the husband he's away
Fetching some timber down in Oseney –
Young Nicholas puts on a playful front,
Goes to this wife, and grabs her by –

NICHOLAS.
I tell you straight – unless I have my will
Of you, my love, I'm going to burst and spill
My life before you here upon the floor –
Oh let me stroke your thighs – it's what they're for –
I have to have you now – O let me come
To you – I'll die! Or else I am undone –

ALISON.
Let be! Let go! Unhand me Nicholas –
Or I'll cry out – Out harrow! Out alas!
Let go your hands – where is your modesty!

NICHOLAS.
Have mercy, lady. Mercy! Pity me!

ALISON.
It may be that I won't –

NICHOLAS.
Pity!

ALISON.
Maybe I will.

NICHOLAS.
Now by Saint Thomas Martyr ye me kill!

She kisses him.

ALISON.
My husband is so full of jealousy,
Unless we wait and do all secretly,
I wot right well I am as good as dead –

NICHOLAS.
Nay! Have no care of him. I'm dull as lead
If I cannot a carpenter beguile.
Am I a scholar? Where've I been the while
But sharpening my wit, to shape mine ends?
Now kiss me close, and take what Fortune sends.

She does. 'He thakkes hir about the lendes weel' – i.e. they grope each other – kiss, and part. He picks up his Sautrye and plays and sings.

SONG.

I have a gentil cock
Who crows at break of day
He makes me rise up early
My matins for to say.

I have a gentil cock
You have not seen him yet
His head is red as coral
His tail is black as jet.

His neck is long and white
His eye is set in amber
And ev'ry night he perches him
In my lady's chamber.

MILLER.

So Nicholas, no longer would he tarry
But doth, in secret, to his chamber carry
Both meat and drink to last a day or two
And bolts the door, and then is seen namo.
He would not answer none, whate're might fall,
How ere the servants shout, or knock or call.
Then says this carpenter:

CARPENTER.

By good Saint Thomas! –
Things standeth not aright with Nicholas.
God shield that he lies dead upon his bed!
This world is so uncertain, so unstead,
I saw a corpse this day to church-yard borne
On Monday last was bringing in his corn.
Robin, go up – and beat upon his door.

Exit BOY.

See how he doth. I do not know what more
To say, or do. Unless we break it down.
Perhaps he's mad? It's this astrominye –
I heard of one went out at night to prye
Upon the stars – some 'horrowscope' to meck –
He fell into a pit and broke his neck.
He didn't foresee that! – Holy Saint Thomas!

Enter NICHOLAS, *pale, as if mad.*

NICHOLAS.
Alas!

CARPENTER.
What! How! How now? What ails thee, Nicholas?
Come cross thyself from evil ghouls and elves –
What do ye seem to see? Here's just ourselves.
Think on Christ his Passion – Look ye down –
Fetch holy water – drench the room around –
Bless us Saint Christ! – Holy Saint Benedight
Bless all this house from every wicked sprite!

NICHOLAS.
Alas! Alas!
Must all the world be lost? All pass away?
Is there so little time till Judgement Day!

CARPENTER.
Say'stow? Think on God, as do men that swink –
Simple men, faithful men –

NICHOLAS.
Give me to drink.
And after, will I tell thee privilee
Certain dark things that touch both thee and me. (*Drinks.*)
Now, John mine host, my levë friend and dear
Thou shalt upon thine honour swear me here
That to no wyght my counseil ye'll betray –

CARPENTER.
Forbid it God! – that anything you say
I should repeat to man, nor wife, nor chile –

NICHOLAS.
Now John, mine host, I will not thee beguile:
I have found out in my astrologee
That all this land shall sink under a sea.
On Monday next 'bout middle of the night
The moon shall rise, and never yet so bright.
Then falls a rain, so wild and without let,
That Noah's flood was never half so wet.
This world, I find, in less than half an hour

Shall all be drenched, so hideous the shower,
All men shall drown, and all the women too.

CARPENTER.
O Alison! My wife! What shall I do!
Is there no remedy to 'scape all this?

NICHOLAS.
What d'ye take me for? Of course there is! –
If you'll stay calm and do just what I say.
Noah was saved last time – this time we three.
Just you and me, and Alison your wife –
Our maid must drown. I can't save Robin's life –
Don't ask me why, God wills it shall be so.
Now go thy ways, and speed thee, go, go, go! –
And get three kneading troughs, or tubs so large
That we may float in them, as in a barge,
Vittels sufficient for a single day –
Upon the next the flood will drain away –
Then hang the troughs up in the rafters high
So none our preparations shall spy –
And bring an axe to smite the cords. You see?
So when the water rises we'll float free –
Over the garden wall, over the stable,
Over the houses' tops, over the gable.
Then we'll be lords and masters all our life
And rule the world, like Noah and his wife.

MILLER.
This simple gull does just as he is bid
And up among the rafters – there – he's hid
Three gurt big tubs, with ladders to them three.
Afore he did he sent his wench away
And Robin with her up to London town
On some fool's errand. Monday night comes round
He shuts his doors, blows out the candle light,
Checks everything to see all is to rights.
Then swiftly up their ladders climb all three
And sitten in their tubs and start to pray.

NICHOLAS.
Pater-noster, Amen!

MILLER.
This Nick'las says.

CARPENTER.
Amen! Amen!

MILLER.
The carpenter replies.

ALISON.
Ahhhh! Men! Ahhhh! Men!

MILLER.
Sighs naughty Alison.
The carpenter does his devocioun
Then falls asleep – for all this bisinesse
Had toiled and wearied him, or so I guess –
About the curfew time, or little more.
In peril of his soul he groaneth sore
And mumbles in his sleep words from the mass –
Out of his tub creepeth young Nicholas
And Alison adoun after him sped.
Without a word they strip and go to bed
And, while the old man snores beneath the moon,
The young are thumping out another tune.
Thus twineth Alison with Nicholas
Straining their limbs to reach each sweet release –
Until the bell for Church begins to ring
And friars in the chancel start to sing.

Enter ABSOLON.

This is the Parish Clerk. Young Absolon,
Since once he clapped his eyes on Alison,
Hath in his heart such lust and love-longing
That oft by night would at her window sing:

ABSOLON (*singing*).
The fairest maiden of this town
Did beg and plead with me
To graften her a goodly graft
From off my sturdy pe-ar tree.

NICHOLAS.
Hush, Alison. Herestow nat Absolon
That chaunteth thus under the window's sill?

ALISON.
Yea, Nicholas. I hear him very well.

ABSOLON.
I grafted her a goodly graft
And did all at her will
And though my pear is graft on her
She will be grafting of me still

What do ye, honey-comb, sweet Alison?
My bonny bird, my sweetë cinnamon,
Awaken, lemman mine, and speak to me!

ALISON.
Go fro my window, Jakke fool, leave me be.
I can get lovers better far than thou
And, could I not, I'd hang myself I trow.

ABSOLON.
Hear me a little, gentle Alisone –

ALISON.
Go forth thy way, or I will cast a stone –

ABSOLON.
Was ever true love so evil beset?

She throws something.

ALISON.
Wilt let me sleep? Or art thou down there yet?

ABSOLON.
Just kiss me once – have pity! – do me right.
I see I'll get not better sport this night.

ALISON.
And if I do then wiltow leave this song?

ABSOLON.
Yea, certës, lemman. Kiss, and I'll be gone.

ALISON.
Well make thee ready, boy. Come near the sill.
Hush, Nicholas, and thou shalt laugh thy fill.

ABSOLON.
I would not now to any lord give place.
Sure – more's to come. She showeth me such grace –

ALISON.
Now hold thy peace! Come up – where artow? – where?
Haste! Haste! Lest all our neighbours spy thee there.

She sticks her arse out of the window. ABSOLON *kisses it 'ful savourly'.*

ABSOLON.
Something's amiss? All rough and shaggy haired?
I've never kissed a woman with a beard!

ALISON.
Te hee!

NICHOLAS.
A beard! A beard! God's corpus, this goes well!

ABSOLON.
Who's there within? Some man? My soul I'll sell
To Sathanas, if I be not awroke –

NICHOLAS (*to* ALISON).
Come back to bed.

ALISON (*shutting the window*).
Be gon ye Jakke!

ABSOLON.
Alas! Alas! Fie on all paramourse!
My hot love's cold – I will kiss no more arse!

MILLER.
Thus was he healëd of his maladye
And evermore would paramours defye.
He weeps as dooth a child that is y-beat
A little while – then goes across the street
Unto the forge – the smith's his friend – Jarvis
Who sharpens ploughshares, fashions harness –

ABSOLON (*knocking*).
Jarvis undo! Now open up, anon!

JARVIS.
Why? Who art yow?

ABSOLON.
It's I – It's Absolon.

JARVIS.
What, Absolon, so early by Christ's tree?
Why rise ye up? Is it some maladee?
Nay! It's a girl he's after – that I'll swear –

ABSOLON.
Lend me that coulter in the fire, there.

JARVIS.
With all my heart. What will ye do with it?

ABSOLON.
Tell ye tomorrow . . . if mine aim I hit.

Goes back, coughs, taps at window.

NICHOLAS.
Who's there that knokketh so?

ALISON.
Who's there? A thief?

ABSOLON.
It is thine Absolon, my sweetë leef.
I've brought a ring of gold, so God me save,
Full fine it is, and pure, and well engraved –

NICHOLAS.
That fool again! I have to have a piss –

ABSOLON.
This will I give ye – if ye will me kiss.

NICHOLAS.
Stay where ye are. I will amend the jape.
(*To* ALISON.) This time he'll kiss *my* arse ere he escape.

Sticks his arse out of the window.

ABSOLON.
Speak, my sweet bird. I know not where thou art.

NICHOLAS *lets out an iambic quatrametric fart, very loud and long on the eighth syllable.*

MILLER
A fart!
As great as it hath been a thunder-dent –
Absolon's half blind ere its force is spent!
But then:

ABSOLON *sticks the glowing implement up* NICHOLAS*'s bum.*

ABSOLON.
Ahaaaa!

NICHOLAS.
Ahhhhhhh! Water! Water! Help for God's sweet blood!
Water!

CARPENTER.
Water? Here comes Noah's flood!

Cuts the rope with his axe, falls from the roof in his tub and his arm is broken.

Ahhhh!

NICHOLAS.
Water! Water! All scalded is my toute!

ALISON.
Out harrow! Oh my love! Out harrow! Out!

NEIGHBOURS *rush in armed and ready to chase off thieves. Confusion and noise.*

CARPENTER.
Ah, Noah's flood is come! We'll drown, we'll drown!

NEIGHBOUR 1.
What saystow?

NEIGHBOUR 2.
Noah's flood?

CARPENTER.
Where's Alison?
Mine arm is braste! I'll drown! We're going to die!

NICHOLAS.
Now mark him not.
He's mad. It's fantasye.

They all laugh at the CARPENTER.

MILLER.
And everyone gan laughing at the strife . . .
Thus swyvëd was the carpenter his wife
For all his keeping close and jealousye –
And Absolon hath kissed her nether eye –
And Nicholas is scalded on the towte –
My tale is told! And God save all this rowte!

ALL.
Amen!

Some laugh, some are relieved it's over.

CHAUCER.
When folk had laughen at this sorry case
Of Alison and crafty Nicholas
The one that most among us might him greve
Was only Osëwald, our poor old Reeve –

MONK.
Is it – er – my turn now? –

CHAUCER.
Because he was by craft a carpenter
And in his heart there lodged a little ire.
He gan to grouche and to complain a bit:

REEVE.
As I may thrive, I say, I could thee quit –
And tell how bleeréd was a miller's eye
If that I list to speak of ribaldry.
But I am old, my jesting days are gone,
My fresh green grass hath withered and turned brown
I'm like an 'Open-arse' – that medlar fruit –
That is not eaten till it starts to rot.

Old men will dance – long as the world will pipe –
Though we are rotting, still we think we're ripe,
And what we can no longer do in bed
That do we talk of – boast of it instead.
Yet I've a mind to show this drunken wyght
How some old dogs still bark – and some can bite.

HOST.
Say forth thy tale then – stop wasting the time –
Look: Deptford! – and already long past prime.
It's Greenwich soon, where many a slut doth dwell,
So out with it – if you've a tale to tell.

REEVE.
This drunken miller hath y-told us here
Of the beguiling of a carpenter –
Perhaps in scorn of me, for I am one –
So, by your leave, I'll pay him back anon.
I have a tale as filthy as his own –
Let's pray God breaks his neck afore I've done.

Four: The Reeve's Tale

REEVE.
At Trumpyngtown, not far from Cantabridge
There runs a brook, and over it a bridge –

CHAUCER.
Oh that's bad – very bad –

REEVE.
Upon which brook there stands also a mill,
And this is very sooth that I you tell.

CHAUCER.
That's worse –

REEVE.
A miller was there dwelling many a day.
As any peacock he was proud and gay.

Pipen he could, and fish, and nettës beete,
And turnë cupps, and wrestle well, and sheete –

CHAUCER.
Sheete? Oh shoot!

REEVE.
There was no man for peril durst him touch –
He bore a Sheffield dagger in his pouch –
And was a thief, like many of his kind,
Filching the flour, and corn men sent to grind.
A wife he had – claimed she was nobly born –
The vicar's bastard, if the truth be known –
Who'd had her fostered in a nunnerye.
She was proud too – and pert as any pye –
Magpie that is – that's what I mean to say –
And for she had this smutted pedigree
Was quick to take offence – insults to see –
No wyght dare call her aught except 'Ma dame'
Haughty she was, her looks full of distain.
They had a buxom daughter, just turned twenty,
And a babe-in-arms, so that was plenty.
The wench was thikke, and well y-grown she was
With turned-up nose and eyes as grey as glass –
Her buttocks broad, her breasts were round and high,
Her hair like golden silk – I do not lie.
This vicar of the town, as she was fair,
His purpose was to make the girl his heir –
Marry her to some fool of noble blood –
And leave his bastard's daughter all his goods.
The Church's holy wealth would, wholly be
Thus kept within his holy familee.
This miller stole a part – there is no doubt –
Of all the wheat and malt the lands about
Produced. And stole he most especiallee
From Solar Hall – the college – Trinitee.
Their Manciple fell sick and like to die
And then he stole the more outrageouslee.
The Master of the college raged and swore
The miller just denied his theft the more
Meekly protesting that it was nat so . . .

In Trinitee there dwelt poor scholars – two –
Testif they were, and lusty for to play
And always up for mirth and revelrye
Upon the Master busily they cry:

ALEYN.
Sir! Give us leave! –

JOHN.
Just for an hour or two! –

ALEYN.
To go tut mill –

JOHN.
An watch the corn go through.

ALEYN *and* JOHN.
Please, sir! Please, sir! – It's just we've never bin.

JOHN.
Please, sir! Please, sir!

REEVE.
The Master soon gave in –

ALEYN.
O thank you, sir!

JOHN.
An may God brekk me neck –

ALEYN.
If't miller steals but 'alf a bloody peck
Of corn, while him an mee's on't watch.

JOHN.
Don't fret yerself, sir – t' miller's met 'is match.

REEVE.
He's called Aleyn – this other one's called John
And somewhere up in Yorkshire were they born –
Exactly where I neither know nor care . . .
But straightway they make ready all their gear,
Saddle the horse, and cast their sacks thereon,
Then plod along the road to Trumpyngton.

ALEYN.

Eh-up! Now then, Simon! How's it going?
How's yer missus? –

JOHN.

How's yer daughter doing?

SIMON.

Aleyn! John! Welcome, lads! What brings you here?

ALEYN.

Our Manciple is awful sick I fear.
With such a wanging ache what's in his head.

JOHN.

He's in such pain – let's pray he'll soon be dead.
Needs must when't devil drives – there's no one else
To bring us corn to grind –

ALEYN.

So we've come us-selves.

JOHN.

Best set to work – as quickly as yer can –

SIMON.

I will, I will –

ALEYN.

We don't have that much time.

SIMON.

What will ye do while all this work's in hand?

JOHN.

Eh-yup, right by the hopper will I stand,
And watch you as you shovel in us corn –
I've never seen a mill at work biforn –
Nor seen the 'opper wagging to and fro.
That's where I'll be.
Aleyn – 'Ow about you?

ALEYN.

What me? I'll stay below here, on me own,
And watch the floür as it's falling down

Into that there trough. Aye, that's what I'll do –
For I've seen nowt of milling – just like you.

REEVE.
The miller smiled at this false nycetee
And thought:

SIMON.
They mean to get the bett'rof me –
But I've a trick or two will blear their eye
For all their study of philosophye.
I'll have their flour in spite of schools and classes:
Great scholars often prove the greatest asses.

REEVE.
Out at the door he stealeth privilee,
Goes to their horse, and doth the beast untie,
And when the horse is loose, he gets him gone
Towards the fen, for there the wild mares run.
The miller gooth back in, no word doth say
And with these scholars passes time u't day
Until their corn is well and truly ground.
And, when the flour is sacked, the sacks are bound.
When John goes for the horse . . . he finds him gone.
And cries:

JOHN.
Out! Harrow! Oh by God's sweet bones!
Aleyn, step on thy feet, our 'oss is loss –
The Master's palfrey's gone – Our 'oss! Our 'oss!

REEVE.
So Aleyn leaves his post and out runs he
The last thing on his mind is husbandree.
And:

ALEYN.
Which way is he gone! –

REEVE.
He starts to cry.

WIFE.
Off to the fen as fast as he may hie
Unthank the fool that shut the stable door.

JOHN.
You silly bugger, Aleyn – that was your
Fault! You should've shoved the peg into the hole!

REEVE.
They both run off as fast as they can go –
And when the miller sees them on their way
He steals some of their flour – makes no delay.

Gives it to his WIFE *and* DAUGHTER.

SIMON.
Well there it is! They thought they'd beat me holler.
That day'll be black when I can't cheat a scholar.

REEVE.
The horse was loose all day – he ran so fast –
Till in a ditch they cornered him at last . . .
Weary and wet, like damp sheep in the rain,
Comes wretched John, and after comes Aleyn.

JOHN.
Alas! Alas the day that I was born!
They'll treat us with contempt – laugh us to scorn.
Our corn is stole – all men will say we're fools –
The Master will – and all the lads int Schools –
An' what about the miller! Weylaway!

SIMON.
You've caught him then? So did he run away?

ALEYN.
Ay, Simon, jest ye on. We mun it take.
But we beseech thee now, for God's sweet sake
Give us somewhere to sleep – summat to eat –
We'll pay you well – it's late –

JOHN.
We're both dead beat.

SIMON.
My house is strait – and room there's hardly any.
But what there is you'll have –

ALEYN.
You'll get your penny.

JOHN.
And get us meat and drink, and make us cheer.
We'll pay our way – we've silver – never fear.

SIMON.
Wife! Send the girl for ale – and roast a goose –
I'll tie their horse – this time it won't get loose.

REEVE.
And in his own chamber he makes a bed
With sheets and blankets fairly was it spread
Not from his own ten foot away or twelve.
His daughter has a bed all by her selve
In that same chamber – there's no other space.
At last they sup, and drink. For some solace
They eat their fill – the ale is of the best –
About the mid of night they go to rest.
To bed the miller goes – with him his wife
Her whistle was well wet – she loveth life!
The cradle at their beddë's foot is set
To feed or rock the child an if he fret.
To bed the daughter goes, and right anon
To bed this Aleyn goes, and with him John.
The miller, like a horse, snorts in his sleep
And from behind his tail come noises deep.
His wife, to bear him burden, plays her part –

Concerto of farts and snores.

A mile away a man might hear them fart,
And snore. The daughter keeps them companee.
Aleyn is wakened by this melodee.
He pokes his friend, and whispers:

ALEYN.
John? Sleepstow?
Did you ever hear a tune like this ere now?
Our corn is stole, whatever he may say,
And we've both had a shitty time this day.
Now all night long, I swear we'll get no rest.

But yet, who cares? All may be for the best –
For, listen John, as ever I shall thrive,
If I can manage it, that wench I'll swyve.
For if a man in one point be aggrieved
The law says in another he'll be relieved.
Now here's my point . . . it's stiff as any pole
This time I'll shove the peg into the hole.

JOHN.
Be careful, Al! Miller's a parlous churl –
An if 'ee wakes, and finds yer swyvin't girl,
He's bound to do us both some villanye.

ALEYN.
Piss on 'im then! I count 'im not a flea!

He goes to the DAUGHTER*'s bed and creeps in.*
A moment's stillness, then swyving.

JOHN.
He'll get his own back now – He's snug in bed:
He'll have the miller's daughter's maidenhead.
An I'll have nowt! – I'm stuck here on me own
Slumped like a draf-sack on me bed . . . Moan, moan! –
And when this jape is told another day
I'll sit there looking daft with nowt to say.
Yet will I try get summat for me pains:
'The man who nothing ventures, nothing gains.'

REEVE.
And up he rises – not a sound he makes –
Unto the cradle – in his hand it takes –
And to his own bed's foot he doth it bear.

MAYLIN.
Oh!

ALEYN.
Ahh!

MAYLIN.
Oh!

ALEYN.
Ahhhh!

MAYLIN.
Oooo!

ALEYN.
A – a – a – ahhhh!

MAYLIN.
No! Leave it there!

WIFE.
Who spoke! Who's there? Is anything amiss?
No? All is well. I'll rise and have piss.

She gets up and pisses. Then gropes in the dark to find the cradle. She doesn't find it near her own bed.

Gone wrong? Alas! I almost missed my way
And got in with the lads – Alack the day!
Sweet Saints above! Then had I foully sped
To lie with these two younglings in their bed.

She finds the cradle by JOHN*'s bed, gets in and tries to sleep.*

REEVE.
She lieth still, and tries to catch some sleep.
After a while this John doth on her leap
And up the good wife layeth on full sore
So merry a jig she's never danced afore –

WIFE.
Oh!

ALEYN *and* MAYLIN *too start swyveing again.*

REEVE.
He prikketh hard and deep like one half mad –
O what a jolly time the two lads had!
Until the third cock – that's one that crows –
Began to sing, and Aleyn up he rose
Weary and wan from swinking all the night:

ALEYN.
Farewell, my Maylin – O me sweetest wyght!
The dawn is come – I may no longer bide –

But evermo, where ere I go or ride,
I am thine own true love, till death me quell.

MAYLIN.
Now, Aleyn, lemman dear.
Go. Fare thee well!
But ere thou leave me, one thing I will tell:
When that thou wendest homeward – by the mill
Right near the entry of the door behind,
Thou shalt thy sack of stolen floür find
Which that I helped my father for to steal.
God keep thee, lover, safe through woe and weal!

ALEYN *attempts to find his own bed.*

ALEYN.
What's here? I've gone all wrong, upon me life!

Stubs his toe on the cradle.

This is the Miller, lying by his wife.
My head is totty from my swink all night.
This is our bed. Thank God I got it right!

Gets in with the MILLER, *embraces him.*

Eh up, John lad. Wake up, and let's get going.
You piggy, you! Just guess what I've been doing:
I have, three times – *three*! – in this short sweet night,
Swyved the miller's daughter bolt upright! –
While you've lain here in a dither all alone –

SIMON.
Ye false harlot! Ye cokkow! What hast done!
Ah traitor! False! Young lecher! Dunghill ye!
Thou shalt be dead – By God His dignitee!
Dost dare disparage – holding in such scorn –
My only daughter? – She so nobly born!

He jumps on ALEYN *and starts punching him.* ALEYN *gets away but the* MILLER *catches him and they fall on top of the* WIFE *and* JOHN *who have fallen asleep.*

WIFE.
Now holy cross of Bromholm help us all!

In manus tuas! Lord to thee I call!
Help, husband, help! Ye hear the scholars fight!
Help! Beat them! Find a staff! Go fetch a light!

JOHN *joins in against the* MILLER. *The* WIFE *gets a staff and hits the* MILLER *over the head.*

Take that! And that! And that! And that again!

SIMON.
Harrow! I die! I perish! O I'm slain!

The STUDENTS *give him a kicking, dress, and run off.*

REEVE.
Thus was the haughty miller well y-beat
And lost his fee for grinding of their wheat
And supper paid both John's and eke Aleyn's
Who thanked him nat, but thrashed him for his pains.
His wife's well swyved – his daughter's cherry's plucked . . .
Lo, such it is when millers grow so false.
Thus was the cheater cheated, as ye see,
And God that sitteth high in majestee
Save all this company both great and small!
Thus have I quit the miller in my tale.

Various reactions from the PILGRIMS.

COOK.
Ha! Ha! Well done! For, by Christ's passiön,
That Miller should have thought on Solomon:
'Beware of bringing strangers in thyn house' –
That's what he says – strangers is perilous,
By night in special – Men avysed should be
Whom that they bring into their privitee.

CHAUCER.
This is our cook, brought with us for the nones,
To boil the chickens with the marrow-bones,
And make us marzipan – pound galyngale –
No one knows more than him 'bout London ale –
And he can roast, and seethe, and broil, and fry –
Make good thick stews – or bake a well-spiced pie.
But sweet blancmanges are his specialtee . . .
A shame about that ulcer on his knee –

This is CHAUCER*'s joke: the* COOK *is filthy and greasy and keeps scratching a huge running sore on his knee, then licking his fingers.*

COOK.
But God forbid that we should leave it there!
My name is Hodge – I'm Roger Hodge, from Ware –
I'll something tell, if ye vouchsafe to hear
A tale of me, that am a poör man.
I will you tell, as well as ever I can,
A little jape that happened in our citee –

HOST.
Oh well, why not, why not? I grant it ye.
And look ye, Roger – look ye – keep on looking –
I hope your tale is better than your cooking!
For many a soggy pasty hast thou sold
And many an old fish pie warmed up from cold,
And many a pilgrim's cursed you up and down –
Out of the bow'lls of Christ – they've spilled their own –
Because you've fed them on some long dead goose
For in thy shop is many a blow-fly loose –
Nay, be nat wrath! – I mean all for the best,
Though truest words are often spoke in jest.

Five: The Cook's Tale

COOK.
A prentice whilom dwelled in our citee
And of a Craft of vitaillers was he
Gallyard he was as goldfinch in a wood,
Jolly he was and dancen well he could –

CHAUCER.
This is dreadful –

COOK.
Well was the wench that with him once might meet

For he was crammed, as hive with honey sweet,
With lust and love and filthy lecheree –

PRIORESS.
I wonder if –

COOK.
This jolly prentice with his master bode
Till he were ny out of his prenticehood
Cursed all the while both early and both late
And sometimes led the route to Newë Gate
To watch some fellow prentice being hanged –

PRIORESS (*appealing to the* KNIGHT).
I wonder if it's quite the thing –

WIFE OF BATH (*to* CHAUCER).
She's been too long shut up in her cloister –
She should get out more – then the world's her oyster.

COOK.
Until one day his master thought him hard
Upon a proverb that saith this same word:
'Well better it is a rotten apple be heaved out the hoord than let it rot all the rem-en – uant.
Well – It's just the same with a rotten servaunt!' – he meant this prentice.
'It is full lesser harm to let him pace than let him ruin all the other servants in the place'.
And so he bid him 'Go! With curses and ill-luck!' . . .
Where was I? – er – Anon he sends his . . . Anon . . . ?
Anon he sends his bed and all his clothes
Unto a mate of his – this wyght he knows –
A sot like him – one of his own foul sort
That loved to swyve all day, to revel and to sport.
He had a licorous wife, that kept – A shop! . . . Just as a front –
But earned her living peddling her . . . 'you know what' . . . swyving and that –

PRIORESS.
That's enough!

KNIGHT.

Right! Just stop there! We've had just about all we can take of this filth.

PRIORESS.

It's disgusting. Disgusting!

HOST.

I know, I'm sorry –

KNIGHT.

This is turning into nothing but swyving and swinking and God knows what else –

HOST.

I know. I –

KNIGHT.

Absolute filth! It'll be sodomy next –

PARDONER.

Will it?

CHAUCER.

Oh come on! It's just a bit of harmless fun –

KNIGHT.

Fun! Fun! You call that fun! And who are you anyway?

CHAUCER.

O, I'm nobody. Just ignore me. I –

KNIGHT (*to the* HOST).

This is your fault –

HOST.

Mine!

KNIGHT.

Yes yours! You should have let the Monk have his turn. So sort it out! Do you hear me? Just . . . sort it out.

HOST.

Sorry . . . Then, my lord Monk, let's have your tale, say I –
Lo! Rochester I see stands here hard by.

CHAUCER.
O do we have to?

KNIGHT.
Will you stop interrupting him!

CHAUCER.
But we need a rest – let's go to the hatch and find
Refreshment – water the horses. There are good taverns in
Rochester – the Bear, the Swan, the Pickled Herring –
Anyway these ladies may need to pass urine –

PRIORESS.
Oh!

HOST.
No, no. I make the rules here.
Proceed, my lord, we're keen to hear your tale –
Something uplifting – nothing old and stale.
O I'll bet my father's soul to a Whitstable oyster
That you're the master when you're in your cloister!

MONK.
I will –

CHAUCER.
Truly dreadful!

KNIGHT.
What's that you say?

CHAUCER.
Dreadful. That's the second time 'cloister's been rhymed
with 'oyster' in as many minutes.

HOST.
Were I the pope – God's bones and blessed blood! –
Not only thou, but every holy man,
However cropped and tonsured were his pan,
Should have a wife. Look how the world's forlorn –
The Church has left the chaff and stol'n the corn.
A vigorous plant must come of vigorous seed
Your layman's only fit for getting weeds –
No!

In bed – just ask your wives – a monk is best!
Let monks restock the herd – weed out the rest.

MONK.
O, come, come, Mine Host! –

HOST.
But be not wroth, my lord, I speak in play
Though many a truth is spoken so, they say.
Now, sir, my lord, and by your patience,
Let's have your story.

MONK.
I'll do my diligence.
A tragedy – that is a certain story –
Is of one that stood in great prosperity
And then fell down out of his high degree
Into misery, and ended wretchedly.

I will bewail in manner tragicall
How some of high degree from heights did fall –

End of Part One.

Interval.

PART TWO

Some PILGRIMS *are asleep, others yawning, all bored stiff.*

MONK.
And hanged was Croesus, proudest of all kings –
His royal throne might nothing him avail
For Tragedy must end in sorrowing –
Her voice hath grown accustomed to bewail
All those whom Lady Fortune doth assail –
With all unlooked-for stroke – the high, the proud.
For when men trust her most, those men she'll fail
And cover her bright face in darkest cloud –

KNIGHT.
Ho! That's enough, good sir! No more of this!
All you have said is true enough, ywis –
Yea, true and salutary – But still I say
A little wretchedness goes a long way
Where stories are concerned. And I for one
Have had my fill of folk Fate hath cast down
From high estate into the depths of woe.
Give us a tale of joy! Of men born low –
Who raise themselves from nought, and climb up high,
And end their days in great prosperity –

MONK.
But that would break the rules of Tragedy!
You can't just –

HOST.
A good thing too, it seems to me.
You'll bore to death our goodly company
With tales of grief, and pain, and misery –
They're half asleep! You drone so drearily –
Give us a tale to wake us up, I pray!

MONK.
Nay, then . . .
Since I've failed to please. I've no more to say.

CHAUCER.
Thank God for that! Well here we are again!
Our Host is not the tactfullest of men.
He has a point, though. While you've been away
This monk's told endless tales of tragedy:
Lucifer, Adam, Samson, Hercules,
Nebuchadnezzar, Belshazzar – both these
Had failed to see the writing on the walls –
Zenobia next, and after that the falls
Of two King Peters, a Duke – Milanese –
King Antiochus, and Holofernes,
Emperor Nero, A Count of Pisa,
Great Alexander, Julius Caesar –
We'd just got on to Lydian Croesus' fall
When, as you saw, the Knight rescued us all
And shut him up. I wonder who'll be next?

HOST (*taking* CHAUCER *aside*).
Now who are you, sir? Can you tell a tale?

CHAUCER.
O don't ask me, Good Host – I'm sure to fail
You worse than ever did our droning monk.
I've simply not the skill. The Miller, drunk,
Knows better how to spin a yarn than I –

HOST.
But everyman must take his turn, and try
To please this keen, discerning audience.

CHAUCER.
But not just yet – I'm hopeless, dull, a dunce –
I need time to prepare – ask this Goodwife.
I couldn't tell a tale to save my life.

HOST.
O, very well. But sooner or later you're for it.
Sir – Man of Law – God give you all his bliss!

Tell us a tale. That's what th'agreement is.
So please acquit yourself at my behest.
Then have you done your duty. Do your best.

CHAUCER.
This man's a judge, discreet, learned, and wise.
Full oft he hath been Justice in Assize –

MAN OF LAW.
Mine host, I'll tell a tale – I do assent.
To break my word was never mine intent.
I will accept the sentence – as is right
For me – a Judge – as any other wyght.
That is our text. The problem, nonetheless –
And here before you I must plead my case –
Is this:
Whenever I discover a good story –
You may be sure – Chaucer's got in before me!

WIFE OF BATH.
Who? Chaucer? Who is this Chaucer everybody's going on about? Speak up – I'm deaf.

CHAUCER.
Never heard of him.

WIFE OF BATH.
Who are you then? I thought –

CHAUCER.
I'm Geoff! Just Geoff . . .

He slides away.

MAN OF LAW.
You must've heard of Chaucer! His feeble skill –
His shaky metrics, and his rhyming ill,
Might serve to make a lewd ballade or two –
Yet hath this drivelling fool presumed to do
Into the little English he commands
The whole of literature! Imagine, friends!
Ovid – Virgil – Petrarch . . . Boccaccio!
Into his witless works the lot must go.
And what he does not write – my levë brother –

In one fat book, he shoves into another.
It's such poor stuff! And – oh so very old!
Why scribble out dull tales? Haven't they been told?
So for my tale how shall I do this day?
I've one may serve – let Chaucer keep away!

CHAUCER.
I have misjudge this judge. And pity 'tis
He's not so witty as he thinks he is.

Six: The Man of Law's Tale

MAN OF LAW.
A Roman Emperor – may God him bless! –
A daughter had whose sweet gentility
All matchless was. Her life of holiness –
And never lived one holier than she –
Was passed in acts of love and charity.
The common voice of every man in Rome,
Unstinting, praised her excellent renown.

There dwelt in her high beauty, without pride,
Youth, without youthful waywardness or folly.
In all her doings, virtue was her guide,
Humbleness had slain in her all tyranny.
She was the mirror of all courtesy!
And Constance was this blessed lady's name –
Her name and nature in one thing the same.

The Syrian Sultan, hearing of her fame
Conceived a love of her so strong and bold
He summoned all his council – in they came –
And all his mind he to those greybeards told:

SULTAN.
Unless I have her I am dead and cold.
I charge you all, that my advisers be,
Shape for my life some sudden remedy.

MAN OF LAW.

Now divers men suggested divers things
Their arguments were cast both up and down
And many a subtle answer offered him.
Some spoke of witchcraft, or compulsion,
But all, at last, reached one conclusion:

COUNSELLOR.

In nothing can we gain the advantage –
Save only this: you must offer marriage.

But in this course there's one thing hinders ye –
I must, in reason, plainly speak my mind –
Our laws and faiths hold such diversity
I trow no Christian prince would, willing, bind
His child unto another of our kind.
Nor would Mahoun, our prophet, smile upon
A union with of that infidel in Rome.

SULTAN.

Then hear my answer, lords. Rather than lose
Constance, a baptized Christian I will be!
I must be hers! I'm lost – I cannot choose!
I pray you do not seek to alter me –
And toy not with my life so recklessly.
I must have her that holds my soul in cure,
No longer in these torments may I dure.

MAN OF LAW.

What needeth greater dilatation?
By many a treaty and embassadree
And by the Holy Father's mediation –

POPE.

Draw near! And list what Holy Church decrees:
Because we would destroy all mawmentree
And bring the love of Christ to heathen lands
We will allow the joining of their hands.
If to these strong conditions they subscribe:
The young Sultan with all his barony –
His lords and tenants – all the cursëd tribe –
Must take the faith of Christ, and Christen'd be,
Submitting them to Rome' supremacy.

MAN OF LAW.

This same accord was sworn on either side –
Constance, alas! Almighty God thee guide!

CONSTANCE.

Now Father, King – behold thy wretched child! –
Thy tender daughter, fostered in thy love,
And ye, my sovereign mother, patient, mild,
Prized over all – save only Christ above –
Constance, your daughter, leaves with ye her love.
To Syria I must go – that heathen race –
Where no more, Father, shall I see thy face.

Alas! Alas! That such barbarity
Should be my fate! But, since it is thy will,
May Christ, who won for us eternity,
Grant me his grace, heaven's bidding to fulfil.
I, wretched woman, will be constant still.
Women must bear all – pain and slavery –
And shall! – as long as men have mastery.

WIFE OF BATH.

O well said! She never spoke a truer word!

CONSTANCE.

Now Jesus Christ our Saviour go with thee.

EMPEROR.

Farewell.

EMPRESS.

Farewell, sweet Constance.

MAN OF LAW.

The mother of this Sultan – sink of vices –
On questioning her son of his intent –
How he'd leave off his pagan sacrifices –
Bestirred herself, and for her council sent
To scheme, and plot, and offer their assent.
And when these folk assembled in her hall,
Taking her seat, she thus addressed them all:

MOTHER.

Lords, by now you'll know – doth not everyone? –
How that my son on point is to reject

The laws of oür holy Alkaron
Given by god's messenger Makomet
But this avow to great god shall I meck:
My life shall rather out my body start
Than shall Makomet's law out of mine heart!

What should betide us from these new laws fell
But thraldom to our bodies – durance vile –
Then pass eternity in fires of hell
Because we have our Makomet denied?
Now tell me, lords, will ye my judgment bide?
And if ye will assent to what I'll say
I'll show these Christian dogs a merry day!

All shout their assent: 'By ye well stand! We shall command our friends! We swear!' etc.

First we'll agree our Christening to take –
Cold water shall not grieve us – not a bit!
Then shall I such baptismal revels make
My son, our Sultan, shall be fairly quit.
For though his wife come clothed in Christ'ning white
We'll send her back bedaubéd all in red –
Fontfulls of water won't wash out the blood!

MAN OF LAW.

O Sultaness, root of iniquity!
Virago! Thou Semiramis reborn!
O serpent clothed in femininity
Like Lucifer of all his beauty shorn!
O seeming woman – that doth leave forlorn
Virtue and innocence through thy foul spites!
O breeder of all sin – O nest of vice!

CONSTANCE *and her* PEOPLE *land.*
They are greeted by the young SULTAN.

SULTAN.

Love, that of Earth and Sea hath governance,
Love, that his hests hath writ in heaven high,
Love, that with pure, and holy dalliance
Halt peoples joins, sets captive peoples free,
Love knit together all this company.

Love, make us both in virtue ever dwell –
Love bind this our accord – And bind it well!

The SULTAN *and many of his people, including his* MOTHER, *are baptised. The* MOTHER *signals for a banquet to be brought in. It arrives. The* SULTAN *starts to eat. This is the signal for the* CONSPIRATORS *to fall on the* SULTAN *and his* PEOPLE *and hack them to death. Only* CONSTANCE *is spared.*

MAN OF LAW.
There was no Syrian – none that had converted,
None that was privy to the Sultan's thoughts,
That was not hacked to death ere he protested.
And Constance have they seized and hot-foot brought
Unto a ship, all rudderless . . . Aboard
They cast her then – Bidding her, bitterly,
Learn, if she can, her way to Italy.

Some of the treasure that she'd brought from Rome
And, truth to tell, vittels in great supply,
They left to her – with garments of her own –
Then cast her out to sail the wide salt sea.

CONSTANCE.
O clear, O bright Creator, pity me!
I pray Ye from the fiend my soul to keep
Since I must drown unmourned upon the deep.

MAN OF LAW.
For days and years th'unhappy creature floats
Upon the ocean, till she comes at last
Unto a mighty castle – where her boat
Upon Northumb'land coast, by storms is cast.
There, on a spur of sand, the ship sticks fast –
Immovable, despite of time and tide.
It was the will of Christ she should abide.
The Warden of the castle, down he came
To see the wreck, and through the ship he sought,
And found the friendless woman, weak and wan
Among the scattered treasures she had brought.
And, in her foreign tongue, mercy besought:

CONSTANCE.
But if ye mean to take my life, then know
Death is welcome. Deliver me from woe.

The WARDEN *and his wife* – ERMINGILD – *revive* CONSTANCE. *They have problems in understanding her, but they are full of pity for her plight.*

I am amazed – I have no memory.
For in these waters wild have I been tossed.
I never more thought human face to see –
My mind, my name, my homeland – all is lost.

MAN OF LAW.
The Warden, and Dame Ermingild, his wife
Were pagans, as are North folk everywhere,
But Ermingild so loved her, as her life,
And Constance made so long a sojourn there –
In orisons, with many a bitter tear –
That Jesu, hath converted, through his grace
The Lady, then the Warden of that place.

Lucifer – seeking ever to beguile –
Angered by Constance and her piety
Bethinking him how he might her defile,
Made a young knight of her society
Aim, hot and foul, at her virginity.

YOUNG KNIGHT (*singing*).
I have a pocket for the nones
Therein I keep two precious stones
And, maiden, if you try them once,
You'll beg them both of me.

I have a jelly tall and grand
It has no feet but it can stand
And it can stab but hath no hand
You guess what it may be?

I have a liquor for to sell
But what it is I dare not tell
It maketh maidens' wombs to swell
Would you have some of me?

MAN OF LAW.

He wooed her hard – but it availed him nought –
Far was her mind from sin in every way –
So out of malice and revenge he sought
To bring on her a shameful death some day.
He seized the time – the Warden being away –
Then silently at dead of night he creeps
Into the chamber where these ladies sleep.

The YOUNG KNIGHT *cuts* ERMINGILD*'s throat and places the bloody knife in the hands of sleeping* CONSTANCE. *The body is discovered. The* WARDEN *laments and wrings his hands.* CONSTANCE *is half-mad. They see she has the knife.*

CONSTANCE.

Alas! Alas! I know not what to say –
Dame Ermingild was ever dear to me –
My very wits, for grief, are all away!

Immortal God who all our sins doth see
From false blame shield and help to succour me.
As I am guiltless of this guilty blood
Be Thou my champion, else I am as dead!

YOUNG KING AELLA *arrives with his court.*

MAN OF LAW.

Aella the King was told of this mischance
And of the time, and where, and in what wise,
Came the ship that brought the lady Constance.
He beckons her – looks long into her eyes.

And the King's heart almost for pity dies . . .
That so gentle and benign a creature
Should suffer so great a misadventure.

For as a lamb towards his death is brought
So stood this innocent before the King.
Said the false knight, that had this treason wrought:

YOUNG KNIGHT.

My life, I swear that she hath done this thing!
Her looks deceive – she is not what she seems.

LORD.
It is not so! –

LORD 2.
She hath such gentleness! –

LADY.
She could not do so great a wickedness! –

LORD.
For we have known her ever virtuous! –

Cries of agreement.

LADY.
She loved Dame Ermingilda all her life! –

LORD 2.
To that bare witness all within this house!

Cries of agreement.

WARDEN.
Alas! Constance, thou hast no champion
Nor canst not fight, thyself! Ah weylawey!

CONSTANCE.
O He that died for our redemption
Shall be my shield and champion this day.

AELLA.
Now fetch your holy scriptures here to me.
Come hither, knight, and face her where she stands.
If ye will swear she hath done villainy,
I will not spare her life for all my lands.
Upon this Britoun Gospel – lay your hand.

YOUNG KNIGHT.
I swear she –

Lightning. A thunderbolt. He is struck down.

MAN OF LAW.
And both his eyes brast out of his false face
In sight of every witness in the place.

VOICE FROM HEAVEN.
Thou hast slandered innocence. Even
In the high presence of Kings – this – and the King of Heaven.

MAN OF LAW.
An unseen hand hath broken his neck-bone
And down he goes – as dead as any stone!

Great was the dread and great the repentance
Of them had harboured false suspicion
Of this simple innocent – this Constance.
And for this miracle, in conclusion,
And by Constance's mediation,
The King – and many others of his court –
Were by God's grace to holy baptism brought.

So Aella wedded her – made her his queen.

Coronation.

ALL.
Donagild!

MAN OF LAW.
Now this King's mother, full of tyranny,
Thought that her curséd heart would burst in spleen
And that to wed so low, an infamy . . .
But masked her hatred in feign'd courtesy.
To Scotland Aella rides to fight his foes
Constance, now great with child, to convent goes.

In course of time a sweet boy-child she bears –
Mauricius, at the font-stone they him call.
The Warden summons forth a messenger,
Writes to his lord the King, and tells him all
The blissful tidings! Blessings on him fall!
Thinking no harm, in order to win favour,
This messenger calls on the King's mother.

MESSENGER.
Madame, rejoice! Now be ye blithe and glad,
And thank our God an hundred thousand-fold
Our lady Queen hath gotten a sweet lad

To joy and bless our Northward kingdom old.
To light our dark, and warm our hearts from cold.

DONAGILD.
Now bless them all – the King, the Queen, the child!
Come! Bring more drink! (This fool must be beguiled.)

MESSENGER.
Lo! Here are letters sealed which tell this thing,
That I must bear with all the haste I may.
If thou would write aught to your son, the King,
I am your servant both by night and day.

DONAGILD.
I don't think so. Not just at present – Nay.
But here this night thou shalt with us abide.
Tomorrow shall ye hear what we decide.

MAN OF LAW.
This messenger drank freely of the wine
And stolen were his letters privilee
Out of his box . . . while he snored like a swine
And substituted very subtilly
With counterfeits – as ye shall see:

AELLA.
The Warden sends . . .
My wife hath given birth unto a fiend.
And in her convent no one dares go near
The mother, or her offspring hideous.
They say the queen's an elf – for none knows where
Her breeding was, nor what her parentage.
All curse the day they gave her anchorage –
Saying she works by charms and sorcery . . .
And every wyght doth hate her company.

He kneels and prays.

Be welcome, all Christ sends for evermore
To me, that am now learned in His lore.
I shape my will to heaven's ordinance,
And bend my heart in all obedience.

Nurture this child, all be it foul or fair;
Protect my wife until my home-coming

Christ, when he lists, will please to send an heir
More fit to rule – better to our liking.

MAN OF LAW.
He seals the parchment – all the while he's weeping.

AELLA.
Place thou this letter in the Warden's hand –
Go with all speed – Go now! Ride like the wind!

MAN OF LAW.
False messenger! Thou slave of drunkenness!
Foul is thy drunkard's breath – addled thy brain!
Thy folly doth betray all secretness –
He hath returned to Donagild again! –
Who doth the King's commands by guile obtain.
Letters are counterfeited as before.
The messenger returneth home once more.

CONSTANCE.
Banished!

WARDEN.
My sovereign hath commanded me anon,
On pain of death, and on my loyalty
That you from out his realm must get ye gone
Else bear the law's extremest penalty.
I am bound on my oath of fealty.

CONSTANCE.
What have I done to earn his high displeasure?
What says he of his boy – our earthly treasure?

WARDEN.
In that same ship wherein you once were found,
Yourself, your son, your goods, by mandate stern
Ye must be put, and cast out of this town –
Out of this kingdom . . . Never to return.

CONSTANCE.
But can ye in no thing read, no thing learn,
What's my offence? Nay, answer not, good friend . . .
Welcome is Christ's will, whate're He send.

WARDEN.
O mighty God! – How can it be Thy will –
Sith Thou art rightful judge – how may it be
That Thou wilt suffer innocence to spill
While wicked folk live in prosperitee?
Alas, good Constance! Ah, so woe is me
That I must thy tormentor be, or die
A shameful death! There is no other way.

CONSTANCE.
O little child – Alas! Where lies thy guilt,
That never wroughtest any sin? Ah me! –
Why will thyn hard-heart father have thee spilt?
O mercy, dearest Warden – Pity me! –
And let my little child dwell here with thee –

WARDEN.
I may not – dare not save the lad, for blame!

CONSTANCE.
Then kiss him once – and in his father's name.
Cold land, and ruthless husband fare thee well!
Now all the world we'll wander at our will.

She sails off. AELLA *returns followed by* DONAGILD, *his mother, and his court.*

MAN OF LAW.
Aella the King comes home soon after this,
Unto his castle – of the which I told –

AELLA.
My child? My wife? Speak! Tell me where she is –

MAN OF LAW.
The hapless Warden feels his heart turn cold –

WARDEN.
At sea – at sea! I've done as ye me told.
Here is your letter – there is your command –

AELLA.
Donagild! I know her hand!
O my mother! No language could express
Thy depth of malice and thy tyranny,

Therefore to hell I send your wickedness
Let fiends record and scourge your treachery!
Fie! Mannish – Fie! – O no, by God I lie! –
Fie, *fiendish* spirit – for I see full well –
Thou liv'st on Earth, thy spirit walks in hell!

He stabs her.

MAN OF LAW.
Now let us stint King Aella for a space
And speak we of the Roman Emperor
Who hearing how his daughter was disgraced,
And all Christians put to cruel slaughter,
Sent forth his legions into Syria.
A noble Senator was in command
Who conquered soon, and all of Syria burned.

And as he saileth home with victory
To Rome-ward, cross the sea full royally,
He met a ruined ship – so saith my story –
And in it Constance, weeping piteously.

CONSTANCE.
Nothing I know, nor where I am, nor why
I am condemned to suffer so much woe –
Nor will I speak his name who made it so.

MAN OF LAW.
He bringeth her to Rome and to his wife –
He gave her to her – her young son also –
And with this senator she led her life.
Our Lady thus delivers out of woe
Long suffering Constance – and others too.
For some years dwelt she in that blesséd place,
In holy works, as ever by God's grace.

King Aella, as he had his mother slain,
Upon a day, fell to such repentance,
And Jesu's pardon hoping to obtain,
To Rome he came, to do his penitence –
Submitting him to the Pope's ordinance.
This Senator, hearing of Aella's fame
Bid him to feast. To feast King Aella came.

Music. A feast.

A young child stood looking in the King's face.

AELLA.
Who is that fair child that standeth yonder?

SENATOR.
Sire, none can tell. And yet he hath such grace –

AELLA.
How came he here?

SENATOR.
O shall I tell a wonder?
From off a wrecked ship – near rent asunder.

AELLA.
And in that ship, sir – was there any other?

SENATOR.
There was one more saved, Sire – the boy's mother.

AELLA.
Let me not hope. O let me not fall prey
To vain phantoms in my head. All reason
Says my wife is lost upon the salt sea.
Hope lends straws for drowning men to seize on –
What if Christ, whom all men may believe on,
Hath brought me here as He sent her to me?
He hath her face! –

CONSTANCE.
Unconstant, lord, are ye!

She swoons.

MAN OF LAW.
See how she swooneth at the sight of him,
See how he weeps and plaineth piteously –

AELLA.
Now God above, 'mongst all his cherubim,
Who sees into my soul – deal mercifully –
For of your harms as free of guilt am I
As is this child – our son – who hath your face,
Or let some foul fiend fetch me from this place!

MAN OF LAW.
And finally, when that the truth was wist
That Aella guiltless was of all her woe
I trow an hundred times or more they kissed
And such great bliss there was betwixt them two
That, save the joy that lasteth evermoe,
There was none like that any creätüre
Hath known, or shall, while that this world endure.
In virtue and in charitable deeds
They passed their days, and nevermore did wend
Till death departed them, this life they lead
Now fare them well. My tale is at an end.
Now Jesus Christ, that of his might may send
Joy after woe, now govern us with grace,
And keep us all until we see his face.

ALL.
Amen!

PRIORESS.
What happened to the little boy?

MAN OF LAW.
Mauricius was made Emperor by the Pope
You'll find his story in another book.

HOST.
Well, what a thrifty tale! – It did us good.
Now by God's wounds, and bones, and precious blood –
Sir Parish Priest – you know about God's lore –
And, now we're in the mood, tell us some more –
By God's corpus, His nails, and blessed Tree!
Tell us a tale –

PARSON.
Ah Benedicite!
What need ye, Man, to swear so sinfully?

HOST.
Oho, Jack-priest! What – would you preach at me! –
I'm sure I got a whiff of Lollardy!
Good men, come near – for by God's passion
Unto you all I make prediction:

Our Parson means us sinful souls to teach –
Some gospel-glossing sermon will he preach –

SHIPMAN.
Nay, by my father's soul, he shall not need!
We've had a belly full of holy deeds –
We all believe that God is Heaven's King
But there is time and place for everything!
Our simple faith comes to us when we're born,
Religion sows the weeds among the corn.
And therefore, Host, I have a tale to tell
A simple one, and clear as any bell –
You won't have need of much philosophy
To understand a tale you get off me –
What's more it's true and modern – judge yourself –
Not from some mouldy book on't lib'ry shelf.

CHAUCER.
This man's a Devon man – Dartmouth I think –
Son of the sea – a good man – likes a drink –
From Bordeaux he ships wine to London Town.
Has he a conscience? Well, one's not been found.
Boozing his cargo on the voyage home –
No wonder trips from France can take so long –
He knows each tide, each sandbank on the way
From Wales to Gottland via Dublin bay,
And every smugglers' creek around Britayne –
I think his ship is called The Magdelayne –

SHIPMAN.
Shove off!

Seven: The Shipman's Tale

SHIPMAN.
A merchant whilom dwelled at Saint-Denize
And rich he was – and so men held him wise.
A wife he had renown for her beautee –

Companionable, but she loved revelree –
Fashions, and clothes, feasting, and gaiety,
Music and show – all wasteful fripperies –
And these are things requiring great expense.
Returns are slight, or none – those compliments
Guests sometimes pay their hosts at feasts and dances –
And that is all. Such shocks to the finances,
When all the bills come in, most men won't stand.
Economy few wives can comprehend.
Pleasures soon pass, like shadows on a wall
Woe to the husband! – husbands pay for all.

WIFE OF BATH.
Why should he not? Why shouldn't a husband pay?
It's right he clothes us – buys our finery –
It's all for his own worship after all –
What man would see his wife look drab and stale? –
For when we dance, and show off some new gown,
The pride – the honour's his and his alone.
For if he can't, or won't pay what things cost
Or thinks it's money wasted – profit lost –
Then someone else must pay our bills for us.
Or lend us gold . . . And that is dangerous.

SHIPMAN.
Can I go on with my tale? Is that all right with everybody?

This noble merchant kept an open house –
The whole world beat a path unto his door
Because he was a gen'rous host – but more,
I guess, because his wife was young and fair.
Among the guests was often staying there
A monk – a handsome man, witty and bold –
Lusty and young – not thirty winters old,
So much at home you'd think he owned the place.
Now this young man – he had an angel's face –
Was so familiar with his wealthy friend
He claimed that they were cousins. In the end
Both man and monk accepting it as truth –
Citing some common ancestors as proof –
Were glad of it as birds are of the dawn.
This monk was called by everyone: Don John,

Trusted he was, and liked by one and all
From master down to meanest page in hall.
One morning, as the birds began their song,
Don John walked in the garden up and down,
Saying his prayers to greet the rising sun.
Into the garden is this young wife come:

DON JOHN.
Benedicite omnia opera Domini Domino
laudate et superexaltate eum in saecula.
Benedicite Angeli Domini Domino –

WIFE.
Don John? So early up? What aileth you,
Dear cousin, are you sick?

DON JOHN.
Nay, nay – not so!
Five hours in bed's enough for any man –
But, dearest coz – you look so pale and wan!
Certës, your man's been hard at work all night
And given you no rest? What? Am I right?

SHIPMAN.
And though he laughed at that full merrily
The thought caused him to blush exceedingly.

WIFE.
Nay, Cousin mine, things stand not so with me –
God who sees all, may witness what I say –
For, by His Son who gave me soul and life,
In all the realm of France there is no wife
That gets less satisfaction from such play.
I may go whistle! O alack the day,
And weylaway that I ever was born!
I've never breathed a word of this biforn –
Nor dare I say to any wyght but thee
How wretchedly my marriage goes for me . . .
Sometimes I think I'll from my husband wend –
Or hang myself . . . somehow I'll make an end
Of all my fears and cares – At last be free –

DON JOHN.

Nay, gentle cousin! God forbid, that ye
For any reason, should fordo yourself!
But may I know – will ye tell me your grief
That I might help somewhat – or counsel ye?
All ye confess I'll hold in secrecy –
For on my breviary I make an oath
That never in my life, for lief nor loath,
I shall not of your confidence betray –

WIFE.

The same I'll swear of yours. Hear me, I say
Upon your hour-book, and by God I'll swear,
Though men threat all in pieces me to tear,
That I shall never – spite of death and hell –
Betray a word of anything you tell.
Not out of cousinage or near alliance
But, verily, for love . . . and for affiance.

She kisses him.

Cousin – O cousin, if I had the time
To tell you all these pent-up griefs of mine,
Then would you hear the legend of my life.
For all I've suffered since I was the wife
Of such a husband – though he's your cousin –

DON JOHN.

He's not! He's not – Nay, nay by Saint Martin,
He is no more a cousin unto me
Than is the leaf, that hangeth on this tree!
I called him so, by Saint Denize of France,
So I might creep into his confidence
And see much more of you . . . Much more of you,
Whom I do love, and ever will be true –
Upon my holy orders this I swear.
Tell me what's wrong. In case he comes out here –
Now quickly, tell me, let it all come out.

WIFE.

O dear my love, dear John, where shall I start?
Full lief were me this confidence to hide,

But it must out, I may namore abide.
My husband is to me the cru'llest man
That ever was, since first the world began –
No! Since I am his wife . . . It must not be! –
I must tell no one how he uses me –
In bed, nor in other private doings –
God shield I should reveal his shortcomings!
A wife should of her husband speak no ill
And nor shall I. I know my duty well.
Save, unto you, a little will I tell:
In bed, so help me, he's no use at all –
He can do less to please me than a fly.
But worse – far worse than that – he's miserly –
And well you know, we women, naturally,
Expect, in certain things, to have our way.
We'd have all so arranged our men should be
Hardy, and wise, and with their money free,
Kind to their wives, and fresh in bed beside.
But . . .
To save his honour and puff up his pride –
I must have gowns and other finery –
And, Sunday next, I find I must repay
An hundred francs I owe – or I'm forlorn.
I had far rather that I'd not been born
Than have his guests to slander mine array –
I'm doing it for him, just as I say,
But, if he finds I've put myself in debt,
I'm dead. But sweetheart you could save me yet.
Lend me the money! Lend one hundred francs.
You'll find I will not fail you in my thanks
If you do this for me . . . Then, love, I pray,
Think in what pleasant manner I'll repay
The loan. I'll do to you what ere you will.
All, you devise I swear I shall fulfil –

DON JOHN.
Now truly, mine own lady dear, be calm.
Let me deliver you from all your harm –
For I will bring for you your hundred francs –

SHIPMAN.
And with that word he caught her by the flanks,
Embraced her lic'rously and kissed her hard.

DON JOHN.
Now go your ways, and say never a word –
Go now – and be as true as I shall be.

WIFE.
Else God forbid, sweet cousin.

SHIPMAN.
Answered she.
Up to her husband's counting-house she runs
Where he hath been since daybreak, casting sums.
And knocketh at the door right merrily.

HUSBAND.
Qui la?

SHIPMAN.
He calls.

WIFE.
Peter, my love, it's me!
Husband? Come out, it's time to break your fast.
O how long must you reckon up, and cast
Your sums, your books, and . . . other tedious things?
There's devil's work in all such reckonings!
You must have had enough of it by now.
Don John is waiting breakfast down below.
Tie up your money bags and come and dine.

HUSBAND.
O dear my wife, how little ye divine
The endless bisynessë that I have.
Amongst us merchants, as may God me save,
There's scarcely one in twenty that doth thrive.
Then must I swink if you are to survive.
We put on cheerful smiles, and a brave face
But underneath we're skating on thin ice.
To Flanders I must go tomorrow morn –
About some goods – I shall not stay there long –

For which, my dearest wife, I thee beseech
To be to every wyght patient and meek.
Look to our goods, be vigilant, take care,
While I am gone, you govern our affairs.
There's everything you need – but I'll provide
This pile of silver for your purse beside.

She kisses him.

They go and quickly hear mass. A table is laid. They breakfast. Afterwards DON JOHN *draws the* MERCHANT *apart.*

SHIPMAN.
When mass was over, tables there were spread.
All of the best this monk the merchant fed.
And afterward Don John addressed him so:

DON JOHN.
Cousin, I hear, to Bruggës will ye go.
God and Saint Austin speed you, and your guide.
I pray you, Coz, be careful how ye ride.
Watch where ye dine – be careful what you eat –
How quickly this hot weather taints the meat!
Cousin, farewell – God shield and prosper thee.
O – one thing ere you go – if it may be,
I pray you, of your goodness, lend me now
An hundred francs – just for a week or two.
There are farm animals that I must buy –
To stock some of our Abbey property –
But brought no gold about me, I confess.

HUSBAND.
God bless you, Cousin – such a small request!
My gold be thine – and use it – make ye free –
My gold, my house, and all my property
Use all I own, dear Cousin, for your ease.
And pay it back whenever ye shall please.

SHIPMAN.
The Sunday next, and while the merchant's gone
Back to San Denize comes this bold Don John
With hair and face all fresh and new y-shave

And to the wife an hundred franc he gave.
But for the gold he doth demand outright

Brutal unfunny swyving.

That he should have her on her back all night.
And so her debt was paid upon the nail
She was well swyved, up hill and downë dale,
Till it was morn. Then Don John went his way,
And bid this wife:

DON JOHN.
Farewell. And havë good day.

SHIPMAN.
In Bruge this merchant finished his affairs.
First home, next Parisward he gan repair
To borr'w of certain friendës that he had
A sum of gold, to add to that he'd made.
And when that he was come to Paris town
He went to see his friend, this same Don John –

DON JOHN.
Cousin! Welcome, Cousin! – Are ye from home ?

HUSBAND.
Now do not think I'm come after my francs! –
I'm here to feast you, Cousin – Give God thanks! –
I have so prospered in my late affairs
We shall not lack of gold for many years!

DON JOHN.
Now God be praised – and still increase your wealth!
I am right glad to see you here in health –
But of that gold you lent me, by Saint James,
On Sunday I returned it to your dame . . .
I put it in her hand, and she it placed
In that small purse she wears below her waist.
You must forgive me, Cousin – sad to say –
And, by your leave, I may no longer stay.
Our Abbot will be gone from town anon
And in his company I must along.
Kiss your sweet wife, and give her one from me.
Cousin – until we meet – I'll pray for ye.

SHIPMAN.
Home gooth this merchant, blithe as popinjay,
For well he knew he stood in a fair way
Above his costs, a thousand francs to make.

HUSBAND.
Now wife, embrace and kiss me for God's sake! –
Straight let us feast and then we will to bed
For we are rich and free – clean out of debt!

More swyving.

SHIPMAN.
When it was day, this merchant would embrace
His wife anew, and gan to kiss her face
And up he gooth and maketh it full tough –

WIFE.
Namoore. Namoore! By God, you've had enough!

SHIPMAN.
But wantonly again with him she played.
Until at last this jolly merchant sayed:

HUSBAND.
By God, my love, I am a little wroth
With you –

WIFE.
With me? –

HUSBAND.
Although I'm loath
To say it.

WIFE.
Oh? Tell me why?

HUSBAND.
Can't ye guess?
I fear you've caused a little coldëness
Betwixen me and oür cousin, John.
You should have warned me, sweet, ere I had gone,
He'd paid you back the gold he had of me.
He put it in your hand, he says, and ye

Did pop it in a pouch about your waist.
I pray thee wife, ye must no more do so –
But tell me always, ere from ye I go,
If any debtor hath in mine absence
Deposit aught on thee. Thy negligence
Might cause me to demand a debt that's paid –

WIFE.
The devil take him, if that's what he said!
A pox upon that false monk's monkey snout!
It's true, I took his gold – I didn't doubt
That you'd instructed him to give it me –
To spend on women's things, and finery! –
He never told me it was gold you'd lent.
But, how so ere that be, the money's spent.
So that is that. What shall I say to you?
You've slacker debtors far than me, I know.
And, should you make demand I reimburse,
Then take what you can find out of my purse.
I am your wife to have and eke to hold
So poke about! You must dig for your gold.

SHIPMAN.
This merchant saw there was no remedy
And as for chiding – that was mere folly
Since that the thing might not amended be –

HUSBAND.
Wife –

SHIPMAN.
He sayed –

HUSBAND.
This once, I'll forgive it ye.
But, by thy life, in future do me right –
Keep well my goods, and keep your purse strings tight.

SHIPMAN.
Thus endeth now my tale, and God us send
To fill all purses, till our life hath end. Amen!

Various responses.

HOST.
Well said, by corpus dominus!

SHIPMAN.
Thanks, mine host.

HOST.
God send sweet winds to waft you round our coast!
Sir, gentle master, gentle mariner –
That monks should make such monkeys of a man!
Nuts for their wives – O dear! – O dear madame!
My lady Prioress, now by your leave,
If I was sure it would in no way grieve
You much – nor cause you, madame, no offence
I would request a tale an if you would.
Would you vouchsafe, dear lady, grant our wish?

PRIORESS (*disgusted at previous tale*).
Gladly.

CHAUCER.
After hot sauce, cold fish.

Eight: The Prioress's Tale

PRIORESS.
There was in Asia, in a great citee,
Amongst the Christian folk, a Jeweree –
Sustainéd by a lord of that countree
For filthy lucre and foul usuree –
Hateful to Christ, and his fraternitee.
And through this street of Jews a man might wend
Access was free – open at either end.

Suppressed laughter from CHAUCER.

A little school of Christian folk stood there,
Down at the farther end, in which there were
Heaps of little children – a little choir –
That studied, in that school year after year,
Such gentle manners, gentlefolk hold dear –

As singing, reading, praying – being good,
As little children are in their childhood.

Among these children was a widow's son
A little choir boy, just seven years old,
Who, on his way to school, would stop, kneel down,
And say 'Ave Marie' should he behold
An image of Our Lady by the road.
His little Ave Maries rang out clear
As had been taught him by his mother dear.

CHILDREN'S CHOIR (*over*).
Alma Redemptoris Mater, quae pervia coeli
Porta manes, et stella maris, succurre cadenti
Surgere qui curat, populo: tu quae genuisti,
Natura mirante, tuum sanctum genitorem,
Virgo prius ac posterius, Gabrielis ab ore
Sumens illud Ave, peccatorum Miserere.

SON.
O what's this song! I pray, friend, tellen me.
I love it so!

FRIEND.
This song, I have heard say,
Was makéd for our blissful Lady free,
As salutation – And her to pray
To be our help and succour when we die.
That's all – or all I know about the matter.
I can do singing – not much Latin grammar.

SON.
And was this song made out of reverence
For Jesus' mother? Say, friend is it so?
Then certainly I shall, with diligence,
Take pains to learn it ere that Christmas go.
If I neglect my primer I will rue it
But for Our Lady's honour I will do it.

FRIEND (*singing*).
Alma Redemptoris Mater

SON (*singing*).
Alma Redemptoris Mater

FRIEND (*singing*).
quae pervia coeli

SON (*singing*).
quae pervia coeli

FRIEND (*singing*).
Porta manes, et stella maris –

SON (*singing*).
Porta manes, et stella maris –

PRIORESS.
As I have said, throughout the Jewery,
This little child, as he came to and fro,
Full merrily would sing, and tunefully,
'O Alma Redemptoris' evermo –
The sweetness had his little heart pierced so –
For going to school he sang it, shine or rain,
And coming home he sang it o'er again –

SON.
Alma Redemptoris Mater, quae pervia coeli
Porta manes, et stella maris, succurre cadenti –

PRIORESS.
But Satan, our first foe, that lying snake,
Who makes in Jewish hearts his foul wasps-nest –
Saith:

SATAN.
Shame! Hebraÿk folk – what – are ye wake!
Why suffer ye to hear this little pest –
To walk and sing wherever so him list? –
For your disgrace to hear his holy rhyme
Offensive to your ears – yea, and to mine!

PRIORESS.
From thence forth did these Jews plot and conspire
This little child out of the world to chase.
An homicide they for their purpose hired
That in an alley had a privee place
And as the innocent did near it pace
This cursed Jew hent him and held him fast,
And cut his throat . . . and in a pit him cast.

Yes, in their stinking sewer they him threw
Where all the Jews would void their stench and stale –
O cursed race of Herod born anew! –
What may your evil ever you avail?
Murder will out! – certain, it will not fail!
This little boy, his little throat all slit,
Ye little think could rise out of the pit!

This poör widow waited all that night
After her little child . . . but he came not –
For which, as soon as it was growing light,
With face all pale with dread and busy thought
She hath at school and everywhere him sought.
Till finally she to the Jewery came
And called upon Our Lady's blessed name.

SON (*from the pit*).
Alma Redemptoris Mater, quae pervia coeli
Porta manes, et stella maris, succurre cadenti –

PRIORESS.
He Alma Redemptoris gan to sing –
So loud that all the place began to ring

That Christian folk that through the Jews' street went
Ran all to listen to this wondrous song
Then hastily they for the provost sent –
Who came anon withouten tarrying
And heard such singing of our Heavenly King,
And eke his mother, blesséd of mankind.
He straightway gave command the Jews to bind.

The little body is carried in procession to the altar in the abbey, singing:

SON.
Alma Redemptoris Mater, quae pervia coeli
Porta manes, et stella maris, succurre cadenti
Surgere qui curat, populo: tu quae genuisti,

ALL.
Natura mirante, tuum sanctum genitorem,
Virgo prius ac posterius, Gabrielis ab ore
Sumens illud Ave, peccatorum Miserere.

PRIORESS.

A shameful death with torments for each one
This provost dooms the Jews:

PROVOST.

They all must sterve
That of the murder knew – and that anon!
I've ne'er before such cursedness observed –
Evil reward, for evil well deserved.
And therefore with wild horses draw them all
And after hang them from the city wall.

SON.

Alma Redemptoris Mater, quae pervia coeli
Porta manes, et stella maris, succurre cadenti

The body is sprinkled with holy water. The ABBOT *arrives.*

PRIORESS.

This Abbot came – a deeply holy man
As all monks are – or else they ought to be –
This little child to conjure he began,
And said:

ABBOT.

O deär child, now I charge thee,
By virtue of the Holy trinitee,
Tell me, what causes thee to sing so sweet,
Since that it seems your little throat is slit.

SON.

My throat is cut – right through to my neck's bone –
And by the natural laws of human kind,
I should by this have been long dead and gone.
But Jesus Christ, as ye in Gospels find,
Wills His glories last, and be kept in mind,
So for the worship of His mother dear
Yet may I sing O Alma, loud and clear.

This fount of mercy, Jesus' mother sweet
I loved always, as well as I knew how,
And when time was I should my life forlete
She came to me and bid me sing aloud –

As ye all heard – and when that I had sung,
Methought she placed a grain upon my tongue.

Wherefore I sing, and sing most joyfully
In honour of that blesséd maiden free
Till from my tongue that grain be ta'en away.
And when it is, thus hath she said to me:

BLESSED VIRGIN.
My little child, then will I come for thee –
When that the grain is from thy tongue y-take.
Be not afraid – I will not thee forsake.

SON.
Alma Redemptoris Mater, quae pervia coeli
Porta manes, et stella maris, succurre cadenti –

The ABBOT *takes the grain from the* SON'*s tongue; the* SON *dies; the* ABBOT *weeps; the body is laid in a marble tomb.*

ALL.
Surgere qui curat, populo: tu quae genuisti,
Natura mirante, tuum sanctum genitorem,
Virgo prius ac posterius, Gabrielis ab ore
Sumens illud Ave, peccatorum Miserere.

PRIORESS.
O little Hugh of Lincoln, slain also
By cursed Jews, as is notorious –
For it is but a little while ago –
Pray, with thy martyred legions glorious,
That God in His great mercy pity us!
And, of His love, grant us His face to see
For reverence of his mother, bless't Marie. Amen.

ALL.
Amen!

CHAUCER.
When heard they of this miracle, every man
So sobered was, it wondrous was to see.
Until our Host –

KNIGHT.
What man artow?

CHAUCER (*moves away*).
Oh nobody, you know . . .
What was I saying? O yes, it wondrous was, and plain to see
That all believed this nun's absurditee,
And trudged downcast, in grudging piety.
Until our host, preferring jolitee,
Sets out to break the gloomy mood anon.

HOST.
Enough of woes! Thou priest! Come here, Sir John!
Tell us a tale to make our poor hearts glad!

NUNS' PRIEST.
With all my heart, Mine Host. It would be sad
For all of us, ywis, if I can't find
A tale of merriment – I've one in mind.

HOST.
Thank God for you, sir, bless your breech and stones!
Let's have a jolly story, by God's bones!

PRIORESS.
Such language! Disgusting!

MILLER.
Disgusting! Swearing like a soldier.

KNIGHT.
Begin, sir! For the love of Thomas Martyr will you begin!

PRIORESS.
I'm beginning to wish I'd gone to Walsingham.

WIFE OF BATH.
Oo it's lovely, is Walsingham.
And ever so much nearer than Jerusalem –
Or even St James of Compostella. Have you been to Rome,
Lady?

KNIGHT.
O for the love of Christ! Jesus our Saviour!
If we're going to listen to the blessed Nuns' Priest's tale –
let's listen to the blessed Nuns' Priest's tale! Or – or – or –
Can we just – just – just –! O I give up! Do as you please –
and leave me out of it.

Nine: The Nuns' Priest's Tale

NUNS' PRIEST.

A poor widow, somedeal stooped in age
Was whilom dwelling in a small cottage
Beside a grove that grew along a dale.
This widow, then, of whom I tell my tale
Since that sad day when she was last a wife
In patience led a full and simple life
For little were her savings and her rent.
By husbandry, and taking what God sent
She kept herself and eke her daughters two.
Three cows for milk she had, and three fat sows,
And then there was a sheep whose name was Mall.
Full sooty was her bower and eke her hall
In which she ate full many a sklender meal –
Of piquant sauce she needeth never a deal –
No dainty morsel ever reached her throat
According to her cloth she cut her coat.
Of milk and of brown bread she had no lack
Eggs as well, and bacon – streaky and back.
A yard she had, encloséd all about
With woven sticks, and a dry ditch without,
In which she kept a cock called:

CHAUNTECLEER.

Chauntecleer.
For crowing, and for song I have no peer.
The merry-organ blowing for the mass
Is not the half so merry as my voice:
My comb is like fine coral, red as red,
And battlemented round about my head.
My bill shines blacker than the blackest jet
Behold my azure legs – there's better yet –
My feet are whiter than the lily flower
With burnished gold my breast is feathered over –
See – in this body – prowess beyond measure.
I've seven hens on which to do my pleasure,
They're all my sisters and my paramours
But one above the rest my heart adores.

PERTELOTE.
I am Dame Pert'lote, fairest of the fair –
Courteous I am, discreet and debonair.
Out of my egg I'd not been seven night
When Chauntecleer first strutted in my sight,
And since that time I have ensnared his heart
In iron chains. He loveth every part
Of me – body, soul – my every feather –
Even my voice. We sing love songs together:

NUNS' PRIEST.
For thilke times – to say so strange a thing –
Both beasts and birds knew how to speak and sing:

CHAUNTECLEER *and* PERTELOTE (*sing the song: 'My Lief Is Faren in Londe!'*).

O star, of which I lost have all the light
With sorr'wing heart well ought I to bewail
That ever in dark torment night by night
My hapless bark all rudderless doth sail.

(*Chorus: Seven* HENS *provide the backing*.)

My lief is faren in londe!
Mine heart is far away at sea
Until I hold him in armen
Until he comes again to me!

NUNS' PRIEST.
One dawn of day so chanced it to befall,
As Chauntecleer perched in this widow's hall
Among his wives, he gan to groan and roar
As man that in his dream is troubled sore.

PERTELOTE.
What, Chauntecleer? Husband awake! Heart dear –
What aileth you, to groan – what do you fear?
Ye been a sorry dreamer – fie for shame!

CHAUNTECLEER.
I pray you – take it not amiss, my dame –
By God, I dreamed! – I was in such a plight –
My heart pounds still – I've had so sore a fright!

This body save from harm, thou sweet Jesu,
And grant such dreams as this may not come true!

PERTELOTE.
Such dreams as what? I pray, husband, expound.

CHAUNTECLEER.
There – in our yard – as I roamed up and down –
I dreamed there came – Dear Lord! – a dreadful beast
Much like a hound, that would have made arrest
Upon my body, and would have me dead.

PERTELOTE.
What colour was't?

CHAUNTECLEER.
'Twixt yellow and blood red.
His tail was tipped with black – and both his ears –
But rusty red the rest of all his hairs.
His snout was small and mean – his glowing eye,
When fixed on me.
For fear I almost die! –
And this it was, perchance caused me to howl.

PERTELOTE.
Enough! For shame, you chicken-hearted fowl!
Alas, I say, for by our God above,
Now have you lost mine heart and all my love.
I cannot love a coward, by my faith.
For certes – what so any woman saith –
We all desire – pray God might let it be! –
To have our husbands hardy, wise, and free,
Discreet, not foolish, generous and good,
Who won't turn pale upon the thought of blood.
We love no boasters . . . Now, upon my life,
How durst ye say, for shame, unto your wife
So small a thing might make you so afeared?
Have you no manly heart, yet wear a beard?
You know what Cato says – so wise a man:
'Dreams yield no truths. Avoid them if ye can.'
Bad dreams are come of nought but over-eating –
Vapours occur, the blood starts over-heating,
And too abundant humours clog a wyght.

Certes this dream that ye have dreamed tonight
Has come of some great superfluity
Of your red choler. So, quite naturally
Being thus chol'rick-red makes folk to dream
Of fiery arrows, hell's flames' glowing gleams,
Or such red beasts as yours. Be positive!
For God's dear love go take some laxative!
At once, I say! – The herbs I'll go and find
To purge you both in front and from behind.
And dread no dreams. I've done. I'll say namore.

CHAUNTECLEER.
Madame, my wife, I've listened to your lore.
You say that Cato bids us take no heed
Of dreams? And yet, in many books we read
By many men of great authoritee –
Greater than Cato is, most certainlee –
Who hold the contrary opinion,
And from experience – each and every one –
Will state that dreams be significations
Either of joys or tribulations.
Lo, in the life of Saint Kenelm I read –
He was Kenelphus' son, that noble king
Of Mercia – how Kenelm dreamed a thing:
A little while before his death, they say,
He saw a vision of his final day.
His nurse explained his dream was sent to warn
Of traitors round him that would do him harm.
But little Kenelm, only sev'n years old,
Would not believe his foes dare be so bold –
So holy was the child. And thus he died
His sister had him killed – 'twas fratricide.
In *Somnium Scipionis* Cicero
Expounds the dreams of Afric's Scipio
Macrobius quotes him too – affirms the truth
That dreams are warnings. And I've further proof:
The Bible cannot lie, so look you well –
What read we in the Book of Daniel?
Did he hold dreams were things of vanity?
No, no! And what of Joseph? There ye see
Where men's dreams sometimes warn – I don't say all –

Of great calamities that will befall.
Great Pharaoh knew that Joseph was no faker –
Who set his butler free, and hanged his baker.
And dreams belong to God, so Joseph says –
I could provide ensamples many days.
But short to say, and in conclusion
I must believe this direful vision
Which seems to threaten me. And furthermore
Upon your laxatives I set no store.
I know 'em of old – potions of venom! –
A plague on laxatives! I do not love 'em.

PERTELOTE.
Then let us speak of mirth and stint all this.

CHAUNTECLEER.
O dearest wife – now heav'n bring us to bliss! –
In one thing God hath graced me in great measure:
When I behold your beauty, sweetest treasure –
The scarlet red that ornaments your eyes –
My manhood rises and my terror dies;
For truth it is that 'In principio,
Mulier est hominis confusio' –
Madame, the meaning of my Latin is
'A woman is man's joy, and all his bliss'.

CHAUCER.
No it isn't!

NUNS' PRIEST.
What?

CHAUCER.
His Latin's way out. Hopeless!

NUNS' PRIEST.
Well what do you expect – he's a chicken?
I suppose you send your own poultry to Oxenford.

At dawn of day he flew down from his beam,
Forgetting all the terrors of his dream.
With 'chucks' he calls his hens into the yard
He's royal now and no longer afeared.
He ruffles Pert'lote's feathers twenty times

And treads her eke as oft ere it be Prime.
His looks are like a lion's, grim and proud
He scarcely deigns to set his toes on ground
'Chucking' whenever any corn he spies
And then come running all his clucking wives.

CHAUNTECLEER.
Chuck, chuck, chuck!

PERTELOTE.
Cluck, cluck, cluck!

CHAUNTECLEER.
Chuck, chuck, chuck!

SEVEN WIVES.
Cluck, cluck, cluck!

PERTELOTE.
Cluck, cluck, cluck!

CHAUNTECLEER *and* PERTELOTE *and* CHORUS OF WIVES *reprise the chorus of the song: 'My Lief Is Faren in Londe!'*

NUNS' PRIEST.
Hearken these blissful birds – O how they sing!
See all the pretty flowers how they spring!

Thunder.

But ever at the end of joys comes woe . . .
God knows how swift all worldly bliss doth go.
A col-fox, full of sly iniquitee
That in the grove had prowl'd for yeärs three
Hath broken through the hedge and lies in wait,
As in his dream our cock hath seen his fate.

CHORUS OF WIVES.
O murd'rer false that lurketh in thy den!
O traitor vile to take the life of men!
O new Iscariot, new Ganelon
But falser far! O Greekish new Sinon
That brought high-walléd Troy to utter sorrow!
O Chauntecleer, accursed be that morrow

That thou down to the earth flew from the beams!
Thou was well warnéd by foreboding dreams
That such a day was perilous to thee.
For all that God foresees of needs must be.
And yet ye took the counsel of your wife –
Though woman's counsel bringeth nought but strife
For woman's counsels brought us first to woe
And Adam made from Paradise to go.

NUNS' PRIEST.
As Chauntecleer about him cast his eye,
Among the cabbage, on a butterfly,
He was ware of this fox that lay full low . . .

CHAUNTECLEER.
Cok, cok!

NUN'S PRIEST.
He cries anon, and up he start
As man that feels a chill upon his heart.

COL-FOX.
O gentil sir, alas, will ye be gone?
Have I offended you? What have I done?
Be ye afraid of me that am your friend?
Now, certes, I were worser than a fiend
If I to you mean harm or villainy.
I often come here, only for one thing:
To say the truth I love to hear you sing.
To hear your voice is all my heart desires.
No angel singing in the heavn'ly choirs
Shows, in his music, more feeling than you.
In years gone by I heard your father too –
My lord your father – God his soul now bless! –
And eke your mother, of their gentillesse
Have often graced my house, and eke my table . . .
As I did them, I'll serve ye if I'm able.
Apart from you, I never heard man sing
As did your father in the morrowning –
Straight from his heart came every glorious note!
He closed his eyes quite tight and cleared his throat,
Then stood up on his tiptoes therewithal,

And stretchéd forth his neck – 'twas long and small –
O sing for me, sir! Sing, for charitee!
Reprise once more your father's melodee!

NUNS' PRIEST.
This Chauntecleer, ravish'd by flattery
So murderous a treason could not see.
Alas, ye lords, you've many a flatterer
Within your courts, and many a losengeour,
That please you well – yea, better, by my faith –
Than he whom soothfastness unto you saith.
Ecclesiasticus damns flattery:
'Beware, ye lords, of all such treachery!'
So Chauntecleer stood high upon his toes,
Stretching his neck, and with his eyes tight closed –

CHAUNTECLEER (*singing*).
My lief is faren in londe! –

The FOX *grabs* CHAUNTECLEER *and carries him off.*

SEVEN HENS.
O woeful day! O day of judgement rued!
O Destiny, that mayst not be eschewed!
Alas that Chauntecleer flew from the beams!
Woe to his wife that took no heed of dreams!
O goddess Venus, Lady of Plaisire,
Since that thy vot'ry was this Chauntecleer
And did thy services both low and high,
Why would'stow suffer him this day to die?

PERTELOTE.
Woe! Woe! Woe! Woe! Alas! Alas! Alas!

NUNS' PRIEST.
O woeful hens, how piteous crieth ye
As when false Nero burned that proud citee
Of Rome – so cried then the senators' wives
For their poor husbands losing of their lives.
Withouten guilt this Nero had them slain –

DAUGHTERS.
Mother! The fox! – hath born the cock away!

MOTHER.

Ha, ha, the fox! Out, harrow! Weylaway!

NUNS' PRIEST.

And up they start, and after him they ran,

A chase.

And eek with staves ran many another man.
Ran Coll our dog, ran Talbot and Garlánd,
And Malkin, with her distaff in her hand,
Ran cow and calf, and ran the little hogs –
All frightened by the barking of the dogs,
And noise and shouting from the angry folk –
They ran them so as if their hearts would break
Loud yelling as the fiends do down in hell –
The ducks quacking for fear they would be killed –
The honking geese all flapped up into trees
Out of the hive there buzzed a swarm of bees –
Ah benedicite! – what hideous noise!
Certes, Jack Straw, and all his rebel routs
Made no such din when slitting Flemish throats
As thilke day when chasing of the fox.

Exit chase.

It seemed as if the arch of heav'n would fall.
But now, good folk, I pray you hearken all –
Lo, how Dame Fortune dasheth suddenly
The hopes and pride of this, her enemy!

Enter FOX *with* CHAUNTECLEER.

CHAUNTECLEER.

I'll tell you what, good sir, if I were ye
I'd turn and curse at them – in mockery.

COL-FOX.

You're right. Good idea.
Now turn again you foolish peasants all!
Pestilence, pox, and piss-pots on you fall!
Now I have reached the safety of this wood,
Yell till ye burst! – 'twill do ye little good.
Farewell, poltroons! Ye may as well retreat –

Slackens his hold.

This cock is mine, to have to hold, and eat!
Alas, dear sir! O Chauntecleer alas!

CHAUNTECLEER *flies into a tree.*

I have to you, I fear, done some trespass –
In as much as you may have been afeared,
When I, too sudden, brought you from the yard.
Please understand, I had no foul intent . . .
Come from your tree? I'll tell you what I meant.
Hmm? Trust me. I speak truth – or God be my foe!

CHAUNTECLEER.
Now curse upon us both should I do so!
But mostly on myself, fall all mischance
If thou beguile me oftener than once.
Thou shalt no more through wicked flattery
Get me to sing, and shut my foolish eye.
For he that winketh when he most should see –
And fecklessly – God sent him friends like thee!

COL-FOX.
Nay then, wind-bag, God send them all mischance
That cannot hold themselves in governance –
Crowing the while, when they should hold their peace.

NUNS' PRIEST.
Lo, such it is when we heed bad advice,
Grow negligent, incline to flattery –
And if ye think my tale's but foolery –
A fable of a fox, a cock, a hen –
Well, my morality is wasted then.
For Saint Paul saith that all that written is,
Is written to reveal some truth, ywis.
Peck up the corn, and let the chaff lie still –
He that hath ears may hear me if he will.
So grant us, God, that we prove all true men,
And bring us to high bliss. And so –

COL-FOX.
Aghhh! Men!

Hunting horns.

Lord save us! The hunt! The hunt is up!

The PILGRIMS, *in hunting gear, with horse and hounds, hunt the* FOX *out of the theatre.* CHAUCER, *as* CHAUNTECLEER, *remains to speak part of his retraction.*

CHAUCER.
I pray you all, that have beheld this little show of tales,
If there be anything that pleaseth you, then thank our Lord Jesu Christ for it,
For from Him proceedeth all wit and all goodness.
If there be anything that displeaseth you, I pray you, set it 'gainst mine own account –
And blame my want of understanding – or my lack of skill –
Not any wickedness of my supposed intent.
For I would have written better had my understanding been better,
And all I have set down, I have set down in hopes of our better understanding
Of the Truth of things – Truth hath been my only purpose.
If, in that, I have failed you, I beseech you pray for me
That Christ may forgive my guilty imagination –
For, I acknowledge, I have strayed too often into many worldly vanities.

For you who wish to come with us to Canterbury –
And hear more tales – of innocence, love and glory
Together with some dunghill filth for seasoning
To make the truth shine bright – well, that's my reasoning –
The Wife of Bath has one of Guinevere,
The Pardoner, one of vice; the Summoner
Will lose his temper when he hears the Friar
Consign his fellowship to hell and fire –
These good folk all shall wend towards Saint Thomas' Shrine,
And, with the help of God, we shall arrive in time.
Go home now, friends – go rest – lay down your load,
And pray for all poor pilgrims on the road.

End of Part Two.

PLAY TWO

PART THREE

The PILGRIMS *are halfway on their journey, resting outside a tavern. Horses are being saddled. A picnic in progress. The* SQUIRE *is singing.*

SQUIRE.

All the long night I lie awake
My cheeks wax pale and wan
And this is, Lady, for thy sake
That loved and now art gone.

All a long night I lay with love
Under a waning moon
I little thought how false she'd prove
Would smile and soon be gone

All the long night I lie awake
My cheeks wax pale and wan
And this is, Lady, for thy sake
That loved and now art gone.

OTHERS (*singing, as an Amen*).

Forever!

DEVOUT PILGRIMS.

Gaudeamus omnes in Domino,
diem festum celebrantes
sub honore beati Thomas Martyris:
de cujus passione gaudent Angeli,
et collaudant Filium Dei!

Exsultate justi, in Domino:
rectos decet collaudatio! Amen!

HOST.

Time for another tale.

CHAUCER.

Who's for a jug of ale?

Duet by the Pardoner and the Summoner.

PARDONER.
Love is soft, love is sweet –

SUMMONER.
Love is kissing when we greet –

PARDONER.
Love is harsh, full of care –

SUMMONER.
Love is cursed most everywhere –

PARDONER.
Love is bliss, love roams free –

PARDONER *and* SUMMONER.
Come hither, Love, to me!
Come hither, Love, to me!

CHAUCER.
Come hither, Love, to me!

KNIGHT.
I'll ask once more, what man art thou?

CHAUCER.
Oh nobody, you know . . .

HOST.
Keeps hisself to himself. What – why so shy?
For ever on the ground I see thee stare –

CHAUCER.
Oh well, that's me –

HOST.
What's on the ground? Rabbits? A hare?
Look upward man! Look merrily! Draw near.

CHAUCER.
I'd rather not –

HOST.
Let him through, Gentlemen. Let's give him space,
So, sir what do ye do? Well, now we'll see.

WIFE OF BATH.
He's quite a poppet – just right to embrace,
For any woman, small and fair of face.

HOST.
He has an elvish look – mischievous 'tis.
Does anyone of us know who he is?

CHAUCER.
I'm in import and export – sort of thing. Wine trade mostly . . .

HOST.
Tell us your tale –

CHAUCER.
O, I'd rather not –

HOST.
Come on. You've put it off long enough. It's your turn –

CHAUCER.
Look, don't think I'm trying to get out of it. It's just – It's just . . . How many times must I tell you – I don't do tales! Hopeless at it!

MAN OF LAW.
O choose somebody else – Let's have the Pardoner – he's seen the world –

HOST.
No, no. I'm the one what decides, and I say it's his turn.

CHAUCER.
This is ridiculous.

HOST.
You agreed. We all agreed –

CHAUCER.
I only know one rhyme –

HOST.
We'll, that'll have to do –

CHAUCER.
No. It won't do at all. Some fusty old Arthurian nonsense –

MAN OF LAW.
O for God's sake! – We don't want that –

CHAUCER.
Of course you don't –

WIFE OF BATH.
I love Arthur and his knights –

HOST.
No, no – that sounds good to me. Yea –
That's good. Come on. We'll hear what we shall hear.

CHAUCER.
Oh very well. You've been well warned. Just don't blame me if I'm . . . Not even sure if I can remember it. My memory's all ungrobbed.

HOST.
Get on with it.

Ten: Chaucer's Tale of Sir Thopas

CHAUCER.
Listen, Lords in good intent
And I will tell you verrayment
Of mirth and of solas,
All of a knight was fair and gent
In battle and in tournament
His name was Sir Thopas
Yborn he was in far countree
In Flaunders, far beyond the sea
And Poppering was the place.
His father was a man full free
And Lord he was of that countree
And all was by God's grace.

He grew into a doughty swain
White was his face as pain-de-main
His lips as red as rose.

Complexion ruddy yet again
And I can say, for 'tis certain
He had a well-shaped nose.

He loved to hunt the wild, wild deer,
Or hawk at herons rivers near,
With grey goshawk on hand.
Then he was good with bow or spear
At wrestling he had no peer
None dare agin him stand.

Full many a maiden bright, in bower,
Languished to be his paramour
When she should be asleep.
But he was chaste and no lecher
And sweet as is the blackberry's flower
That berries bear in heaps.

Sir Thopas pricked through forests deep
Therein was many a wild, wild beast
Yea, buck, and fox, and hare.
And as he pricketh North and East
I tell you true, he had at least,
A bucketful of care.

The birdies sang, don't say me nay,
The sparrowhawk and popinjay
A joy it was to hear.
The thrustlecock made eke his lay
The woodpigeon upon the spray
Sang bright and loud and clear.

MAN OF LAW.
What did I tell you?

CHAUCER.
Sir Thopas fell to love-longing
Because he heard the throstle sing,
And pricked like he were mad.
His horse because of all this pricking
So sweated that men out might wring him
His flanks were flecked with blood.

This good knight yelled 'Ah, Saint Marie
Ah what is love? What's wrong with me?
I am in love so sore!
I dreamed all through the night, pardee,
An elf-queen should my lover be
Yea, yea, yea, yea some more.

That elf-queen will I love, ywis
For in this world no woman is
Worthy to be my mate.'
Then came a giant bold and fierce
Sir Oliphant his name he gives
Our good knight didn't wait.

Sir Thopas did retreat full fast
While great big stones the giant cast
Out of a sort of sling.
But clean away got good Thopas
And it was all through God's good grace
And through his fast riding.

Lo, that completes my poem's first fit
And if you want some more of it
I'll do the best I can:

MAN OF LAW.
O for God's sake no more –

CHAUCER.
Now shut your mouth, for charitee
Both knight and knave and lady free
And hearken to my tale.
There's twelve more fits to go, you'll see,
Of love, and fights, and chivalree
To tell them I'll not fail –

HOST.
I think –

CHAUCER.
His mighty steed he well bestrode
And off he galloped down the road
As spark cracks out from fire –

KNIGHT.
Really this is –

CHAUCER.
Upon his crest he bore a tower
And therein sticked a lily flower
God shield him, and inspire –

HOST.
Namoore of this for God his dignitee!

CHAUCER.
He drank some water from a well
As did the good knight Percivell
And all the while he sang this song:
I can't get no satisfac-tioun! I can't get no satisfac – tioun –

HOST.
Stop!

ALL.
Shut up! Rubbish! *etc.*

HOST.
Mine ears are aching from thy drasty speech
'Tis nought but doggerel –

CHAUCER.
Oh well!
And what if it is? How would you know? Eh?
Why stop me in full flight? More than the rest?
I'd just got going – I'm doing my best –

HOST.
By God, to tell you plainly – at a word –
Your drasty rhyming isn't worth a turd.
You're nothing but a waste of all our time –
So, sir, my judgement's final – no more rhyme!

PARDONER *and* SUMMONER.
Love is soft, love is sweet –
Love is kissing when we greet –

PARDONER.
Love is harsh, full of care –

SUMMONER.
Love is cursed most everywhere –

PARDONER.
Love is bliss, love roams free –

PARDONER *and* SUMMONER.
Come hither, Love, to me! Come hither, Love, to me!

CHAUCER.
This red-faced harlot is a Summoner
And this – his gentil friend – a Pardoner
Who from his travels has at last come home –
By way of Flaunders – from the Court of Rome.
You see that leather wallet that he's got?
Packed full of Papal pardons piping hot.
You heard his voice? A goat's voice, light and clear –
I'd say that he's a eunuch, or a queer.
But at his job – from Berwick down to Ware,
They've never met a better Pardoner:
At bare-faced lying he cannot be beat –
He has a bit of pillowcase or sheet
The which he's claiming was Our Lady's veil;
Another bit's the gobbet of the sail
Saint Peter hoisted, when he walked the waves –
Or tried to – until Jesus Christ him saved.
He has a cross of lead, a bag of stones,
And old glass bottles stuffed with piggy's bones,
And with these 'relics' he makes more in gold
Than all the fools he cheats have ever told –

HOST.
Thou, Bel-ami – thou, Pard'ner – do your best
Tell us of mirth or japes at once – some jest –

PARDONER.
Well, if you wish. Why not? It shall be done!
But first I'll take a drink – and eat this bun.

SUMMONER *passes him a cup of ale.*

KNIGHT.
But nothing filthy, nothing lewd, say I.

PRIORESS.
Nay, let him tell no tales of ribaldry.
Tell us some moral tale our hearts to cheer –
Uplifting stuff – that's what we want to hear.

Eleven: The Pardoner's Tale

PARDONER.
A moral tale? Well then . . .
In Flaunders once there was a company
Of rich young men well versed in foolery –
Riots and gaming, brothels, ale-house bars –
Who with the noise, of lutes and their guitars
Would dance, and waste their money night and day,
And eat and drink – and not know when to say:
'Hold, stop – enough!' . . . The devil they'd befriend.
The oaths they used would make hairs stand on end –
O what a grisly thing to hear them swear! –
Our blessed Saviour's body they would tear –
As if those Jews had rent Him not enough –
And each of them at others' sins would laugh.
O if we knew how many maladies
Follow excess and wicked gluttonies!
O wretched sots to make your guts a god!
O guts! O belly! O foul, stinking cod
Brimfull of dung! O rotting filthy mound –
From both your ends how noxious is the sound!
O drunken man, disfigured is thy face,
Sour is thy breath, repulsive thine embrace!
Thy tongue is tied, thy common sense hath flown,
And no man's counsel keep'st – not least thine own.
Ye lurch from side to side like some stuck swine.
For God's sake, man! Just keep away from wine.

These rioters – three – of which I'm going to tell,
Long ere the dawn chimes rang from steeple bell,
Were sitting in a tavern, soaked in drink,

And as they drank they heard the death-bell clink
Beforn a corpse, was carried to his grave.
So one of them gan calling to his knave:

RIOTER 1.
Hey you! Go quick – and ask 'em readily
What corpse is this that passeth here foreby.
And look that thou remember his name well.

BOY.
Sir, by your leave, ye have no need to yell.
I've known who that corpse was a good two hours.
He was – (*Aside.*) I'm glad to say – a mate of yours
And suddenly was he slain – just this last night,
For, drunk, as he sat in his bench upright
There came a privvy thief who men call Deäth,
That, in this country, all the people sleey'th.
And with his spear he smote his heart in two,
And went his way withouten wordës moe.
A thousand hath he slain this pestilence –
And masters – ere ye come in his presence –
Methinketh that it were good policy
To be on guard 'gainst such an advers'ry.
Be ready for to meet him evermore –
Or so my mother taught. I'll say namore.

TAVERNER.
The child speaks true, for Death's been slaying this year
Within that village – 'bout a mile from here –
Men, women, children, day on day, on day.
Perhaps that's where he lives – Best keep away,
Lest that he does ye some dishonour.

RIOTER 1.
Yea? To meet with him is such a danger?
By God's nailed arms and bloody body beat,
I shall go seek him out from street to street –
I make this vow, by Goddë's holy bone, –
We three are each for all, and all for one –
Hold up all, your hands! Smite each the other!
Swear we'll all be one another's brother –
And then we'll seek and slay this traitor Death –

He shall be slain – he that so many sleey'th!
And – by the devil's arse – ere it be night!

RIOTER 2.
Together then! Let's all our true loves plight! –

RIOTER 3.
To live and die, each one of us for t'other –

RIOTER 1.
Now are you each to me a true-born brother!

They go in search of death, swaying, swearing, lurching and singing.

ALL THREE (*singing*).
Our King Edward slew the Frenchies
Deo Gracias!
Our brave sodjers swyved their wenches!
Kiss the devil's arse!

Our King Edward chased the fox
Deo Gracias!
Our brave sodjers caught the pox
Kiss the devil's arse!

Our King Edward pissed on France
Deo Gracias
Our brave sodjers shat their pants
Kiss the devil's arse!

RIOTER 1.
Who's this on't road? Hey you – so who are ye?

OLD MAN.
Good morrow, lordings. Now may God you see!

RIOTER 1.
What churl are ye, with such a sorry grace?

RIOTER 2.
Why artow all wrapped up – except thy face?

RIOTER 3.
Why starest thou so hard at my visage?

RIOTER 1.
Why livést thou so long in such great age?

OLD MAN.

I live so long because I cannot find
A man – nay though I walked to furthest Ind,
Neither in cities, nor in no villäge –
Willing to change his youth for my great age.
And therefore must I keep my old bones still
As long a time as it shall be God's will.
Not even Death, alas, will take my life.
I stumble onwards, all my mind in strife,
And on the ground, which is my mother's gate,
I knock, thus – with my staff, early and late
And cry 'O dearest mother let me in!
Lo how I vanish – blood, and bones and skin.
Alas! When may my poor bones be at rest?
Mother, I'd give those fine robes in the chest
That in my chamber hath so long time bin
For one poor clout to wrap my body in!'
But yet, alas, she won't do me that grace,
For which full pale and sunken grows my face.
But, sirs, in you it is no courtesy
To offer an old man such villany,
Unless he gives offence in word or deed.
In holy writ – it's there that you may read:
'Give place to old men, hoary in the head,
Show them respect.' And it's been truly said:
'Do unto old men no more hurts than you
Would wish upon yourselves when you're old too.'
Now God be with you all! I've far to go –

RIOTER 1.

Nay, ancient churl, by God thou shalt not so –
Thou partest not so lightly, by Cock's breath!
Did'st thou not speak of this false traitor Death –
Know what I think? I think you are his spy.
Tell where he is, lest thou it dear abye.
Dear God! Now by the Holy sacrament! –
This Death and you have both the same intent –
To steal us young folks' lives – you thieving swine –

OLD MAN.
Nay then, young sirs – if ye be so inclined
To find out Death, turn up this crooked way
For in that grove I left him, by my fey,
Under a tree. And there he doth abide.
For all your boasts, and threats, he will not hide.
See ye that oak? Right there ye shall him find.
Now through Our Lord, that bought again mankind,
May you amend!

The three of them draw their swords and run to the tree yelling war-cries, but stop in astonishment when they reach the tree.

RIOTER 1.
What's here?

RIOTER 2.
What's there?

RIOTER 3.
What's where?

RIOTER 1.
What have I found?

RIOTER 2.
It's gold!

RIOTER 3.
They're florins –

RIOTER 1.
Just left on the ground.
There must be nigh eight bushels when all's told –

RIOTER 2.
Florins!

RIOTER 3.
Gold? Gold!

RIOTER 2.
We're rich!

RIOTERS 1 *and* 2.
Gold coins! Bright gold!

PARDONER.
No more thoughts of Death.
The worst of them – when he had caught his breath,
Said:

RIOTER 1.
Brothers, draw near. Take heed of what I say –
I am the wisest, though I jest and play:
Fortune hath flung florins so liberally
To waste our lives in mirth and jollity –
So lightly as they come, we will 'em spend –
Who guessed this morning, that at this day's end,
We'd all be rich – so high in Fortune's grace?
Now . . .
How might the gold be carried from this place,
Home to my house – or else to one of yours? –
For well you know, we found it so it's ours –
But only when it's under lock and key
May we rejoice. It can't be moved by day –
How could we prove it's ours? There is no way –
'They're thieves and cut-throats' everyone would say,
And for our own treasure they'd hang us all.
It must be done by night, if done at all,
As silently and slyly as we may.
Wherefore, I urge we draw straws right away –
The one who wins the draw, the lucky swine,
Shall run to town and bring us food and wine.
The other two will stay and watch the gold
And then, when it grows dark, if our luck hold,
All three of us will carry it away –
Wherever we think best. What do you say?

RIOTER 3.
Agreed. Cut me your straws. How will it fall?

PARDONER.
The draw fell to the youngest of them all,
And off he went towards the town anon.

RIOTER 3 (*running off*).
Our King Edward died one day.
Deo Gracias!

RIOTERS 1, 2 *and* 3.
Down to hell he made his way.
And kissed the devil's arse!

RIOTER 2.
Thou knowest well thou art my brother sworn?
Now as it haps our other brother's gone
And here lies all this gold in great plentee
And we must share it out between us three
Unless . . .

RIOTER 1.
Unless?

RIOTER 2.
Unless by some means I could shape it so
That it was shared out just between us two.
Would I have done a friendly turn by thee?

RIOTER 1.
Well yes – But I can't see how that may be.
He knows too well the gold's left with us twain.
What can we say when he comes back again?

RIOTER 2.
Can you be secret? If I could trust you
I'd tell you here – in plainest words and few –
What we shall do to bring this thing about.

RIOTER 1.
You know that you can trust me – out of doubt.
How could one brother t'other one betray?

RIOTER 2.
There's two of us. And I can surely say
That two of us are stronger far than one.
When he is back with drink, and sitting down,
Wrestle with him, and roll – give him a fall –
And I shall ryve him through – sides, guts and all.

And with thy dagger look thou do the same.
We share the gold, the youngster's out the game.

PARDONER.
This youngster, then, was wand'ring through the town
And in his mind was turning up and down
The beauty of those florins, new and bright.

RIOTER 3.
Oh Lord!

PARDONER.
Quod he –

RIOTER 3.
If only that I might
Keep all this treasure to myself alone,
There is no lad that lives under the throne
Of God would live so merrily as I!

He goes to an APOTHECARY.

Apothec'ry, I pray'ee – will ye sell
Some poison? I've a bunch of rats to quell –

APOTHECARY.
Rats? –

RIOTER 3.
And there's a pole-cat lurking in my wood,
That's killed two capons – so I'm out for blood.

APOTHECARY.
In all the world there is no creäture
That eats or drinks part of this confiture –
A dose as small as is a grain of corn –
And then can live to see another morn.
Yea, starve he must, and in a lesser while
Than it would take a dog to run a mile.

RIOTER 3.
O that's for me, then!

PARDONER.
He took the poison in a box and ran
Into the next street to another man

And borrowed of him these large bottles – three,
And into two his poison pouréd he,
Keeping the third one clean for his own drink.

RIOTER 3 *runs back, humming or whistling the song's tune, with food and three bottles to the other two. He sits down excited and exhausted, and begins to set out the food.* RIOTER 1 *starts the shove and play with him. They wrestle.* RIOTER 2 *stabs him.* RIOTER 1 *pulls out his dagger and stabs him as well.*

RIOTER 2.
Now let us sit and drink, and make us merry,
And afterwards we will his body bury.

They drink to their success.

PARDONER.
Thus fell all three, like Lucifer from pride –
Alas! Mankind, how may it thus betide
That to thy Creator – He whom thee wrought,
And with his precious blood ye sinners bought –
Thou art so false, and so unkind, Alas!
May God forgive your stubborn wickedness,
And keep you from the sins of drink and greed . . .

If He will not, my pardons then you'll need.
I've relics and I've pardons – here, you see? –
The Pope in Rome, entrusted them to me
So that I may your spotted souls scrub white
If you've no gold then silver is all right.
Look here! I write your names on this scroll – so –
And into Heav'n's bliss you straight will go.
I think that this our Host should first begin
Since that he most envéloped is in sin.
Kneel down, mine host, pay up, it's quickly done,
And you shall kiss my relics – every one.

HOST (*he's been drinking*).
And you shall kiss mine arse ere I kiss yours!
Next thing you know, he'd have me kiss his drawers
And swear they were the shirt of some old saint –
Yea – though his shitty arse daubed on the paint!

Now by the cross that Holy Helen found
If I could get your bollocks in my hand,
I'd cut 'em off, and pack 'em in pigs' shit,
And bottle 'em, and make a shrine of it!

KNIGHT.
No more of this, I think that's quite enough.
Your manner, gentil host, is far too bluff.
Sir Pardoner, look up, be of good cheer
And you, mine Host – I'll have no quarrels here.
I pray you – come and kiss the Pardoner.
And Pardoner – I pray you, sir, draw near.
And as we've done before let's laugh and play.

CHAUCER.
And so they kissed, and we rode on our way . . .

HOST.
There's no honour left – love and friendship's cold,
This world's turned all to grasping, greed and gold.
Come, Doctor, sir – upon you lights mine eye.
Give us a tale to make us laugh or cry.

PHYSICIAN.
Gladly.

CHAUCER.
And speaking of gold . . .
A Doctor – of Physic and of surgery,
Also well grounded in astronomy.
He keeps his patients waiting hours and hours
Until the planets turn and lend their powers,
And knows the cause of every malady.
The more the patients wait, the more they pay
And then he sends them to th'apothec'ry,
Where they pay more! – for drugs and remedies.
Our Doctor takes a cut of what they're charged
And thus his store of gold is much enlarged.
A patient must be bled, or leeched, we're told.
The physick Doctors give *themselves* is gold.

Twelve: The Physician's Tale

PHYSICIAN.

There was, as telleth Titus Livius,
A knight that callėd was Virginius
Loved for his honour and his worthiness
Strong in his friends, possessed of great richesse.

VIRGINIA *plays the lute.*

He had a daughter, chaste and virtuous
Famed for her beauty and her gentillesse,
A maid of fourteen years – Nature's delight
That painted her complexion lily-white,
And rose-bud red. Phoebus hath gild her hair
In streams turned golden by his radiance fair.
Pallas Athene gave abundantly
Of wisdom, fortitude, and modesty
To this sweet maid – flow'r of virginity;
In spirit, as in body, pure was she.

O that these young girls you may see today
Would make of her a mirror, let me say,
Instead of keeping evil company
Wherein they learn to sin excessively
At feasts, and revels, and unseemly dances –
Merely occasions for dalliances.
Such things make children oftentimes to be
Too ripe too soon, and brazen, as we see.
You that are fathers – and you mothers too –
All that have care of children – one or moe –
Take better charge of their surveyance
While that they be under your governance.
Where are they now? And what are they doing?
Who are they with? How may you be knowing?
Beware, lest by ensample of your living
Or by your negligence in chastising
They're brought to grief. For me – I dare well sayn
If they should perish, 'tis yourselves to blame:
Under a shepherd soft and negligent
The wolf finds many a sheep and lamb to rend.

Let this warning suffice, no more I'll say,
But come back to my tale without delay.
This maid, upon a day went all alone
Towards a temple, in the town of Rome.

APPIUS.
Who is that maid who walks so modestly?
She must be mine, whatever men may say.

PHYSICIAN.
This is Appius, gov'nour of the borough,
A great Justice, supposed a man of honour –
But when his eye upon the maiden fell
His heart was changed withal, his mood as well.
So stricken was he with her loveliness
The fiend filled all his thoughts with uncleanness.

APPIUS.
And yet I know not, by no means nor mead,
How it may be that my foul lust may speed.
Her father's strong in friends, and also she
Confirméd in her virgin sov'reignty.
Try as I might, I fear I'll never win
That perfect body to the ways of sin.
And yet I must. Ho, Claudius, come here.

CLAUDIUS.
Now what's your will, my lord?

APPIUS.
Lend me your ear.
That you shall secret be, I will ensure:
Reveal my words to any creäture
And you must lose your head. Do you agree?

CLAUDIUS.
I do, my lord.

APPIUS.
I will have secrecy.
But if you shapen my conspiracy –
In every point, perform it subtillee,
And make a passage for my lechery,
I'll give you gifts that precious are and dear.
Draw close to me, no other wyght must hear.

PHYSICIAN.

And so false Appius, says Livy's story,
As was his wont, sat in his consistory,
Giving his judgement on some trifling case
When Claudius, that churl, burst in the place,
Crying:

CLAUDIUS.

Justice! Great judge, and if you will,
Now do me right upon this piteous bill –
Hear my complaint against Virginius!
And if he dares to say it is not thus
I will bring proof and many witnesses
To say my bill is truth and righteousness.

APPIUS.

Hold, fellow, hold. I may not give sentence
Upon a Roman lord in his absence.
Officers – Let Virginius be brought –
With all the haste ye may – into my court.
When he is come, your plea I'll gladly hear.
Thou shalt have right – there's no injustice here.

VIRGINIUS.

My lord and judge, I come to know your will.

APPIUS.

Then stand and hear this fellow read his bill.

CLAUDIUS.

The justice of my case this court shall hear.
To you, my lord, sir Appius most dear,
Shall prove your humble servant Claudius
How that a knight – this same Virginius –
Against the law, against all equity,
Holdeth by force, against the will of me,
My servant, one that is my thrall by right,
Which from my house was stole upon a night,
While yet she was but young. This will I prove.
By witnesses' sworn statements I'll remove

Handing depositions up.

All claim that she's his daughter as he says.

She is my thrall. And so, my lord, I pray,
Yield me my slave, if that it be your will.
Grant justice, worthy judge – accept my bill.

APPIUS.
Virginius?

VIRGINIUS.
What, mockery is this?
And must I answer it, Lord Appius?
What he hath spoke is false, as all Rome knows –
I'll bring a thousand witnesses – all those
Will prove how much this villain is a liar.
Let me go home. Our time is wasted here.

APPIUS.
Nay – not so hasty, sir. Your advers'ry
By these sworn oaths hath proved conclusively
He hath the right of it.

VIRGINIUS.
Now gods, hear me –

APPIUS.
They may, but I will not! I say to ye
I'll hear no word of you Virginius –
But straightway give my judgement. It is thus:
I deem anon this man shall have his slave.
Thou shalt no longer in thine house her save.
Go bring her here, and put her in our ward.
Soldiers go with him. See I am obeyed.

PHYSICIAN.
And when this worthy knight Virginius
Through practice of this Justice Appius
Saw that he must, by force, his daughter give
Unto the judge in lechery to live,
He goeth home, and sits down in his hall
And bids at once some to his daughter call.
And when she comes, his face like ashes cold,
With downcast eyne he doth her face behold.

VIRGINIUS.
Daughter, my love, Virginia, precious name,

There are but two ways – either death or shame.
One must thou suffer, though thine innocence
Shines like the sun. Thou hast done no offence.
Nor never sinned in thought, nor deed, nor word
Thou art the last should die upon my sword.
O hapless child – O all my happiness! –
Fixed ever in my heart. Forgetfulness
Will never part us while I yet have breath,
Though life and joy are ended with thy death.
O gem of chastity! – in patiënce
Take thou thy death, for death is my sentence –
For love, not out of hate, I must thee kill!
Alas, false Appius that judged so ill
Ever saw thy face! Come, bid me goodbye.

VIRGINIA.
O mercy, dearest father! Must I die?
Is there no grace? Is there no remedy?

VIRGINIUS.
No, certes, daughter mine, our enemy
Hath set a snare for us and we are ta'en.

VIRGINIA.
Then give me death, ere ever I have shame.
Do with your child your will – And, in God's name,
I count it blessing that I die a maid.
Strike softly, father. Heaven lend her aid –

VIRGINIUS.
She swoons. She swoons . . .

Cuts off her head, goes and throws it at the feet of APPIUS.

APPIUS.
Aghhhhh! Take him and hang him! Hang him on a tree!

FIRST ROMAN.
Now save the knight! In love and for pitee!

SECOND ROMAN.
And hang the judge for his iniquitee!

PHYSICIAN.

They threw him in a dungeon deep and strong
Where, in remorse, he hanged himself anon.
And to the judgement of Virginius
They dragged this wretched wyghte, false Claudius.

VIRGINIUS.

No, let him go. He was mere instrument
Of other's lust. I doom him banishment.

PHYSICIAN.

Here you may see how sin hath his reward.
No man knows how, but God will keep his word:
'Vengeance is mine! I will your sins repay!'
Sometimes the worm of conscience gnaws away
A sinner's life, and only he knows why –
Save only God who all our sins doth spy.
Be sure the blow will fall. Though where and when
Is hidden from both fools and learned men.
But it will come. Therefore this counsel take:
Forsake your sins, lest you your God forsake.

HOST.

Now by Coggs's wounds, I'm wood! As wood as wood!
Harrow! By God, and by his nails and blood!
False judges and false witnesses to boot!
My curses on them – tread them underfoot!
As shameful death as may a man devise
Fall on all Judges and on their assize!
Alas that poor sweet maid – and was she dead?
Better ten thousand lawyers died instead.
Now truly, let me say, my master dear,
That was a piteous tale for us to hear.
But nonetheless, press on, and God bless you,
And bless thy urinals, and jordans too.
My heart is broke for pity of this child . . .

WIFE OF BATH.

Let women be the judges! They are mild
In judgement, fair – do all for justice' sake.
Leave judgement to men? – See the mess they make!

CHAUCER.
This widow comes from somewhere close to Bath.
By sad misfortune she has turned quite deaf.

WIFE OF BATH.
What's he saying?

CHAUCER.
Nothing, nothing!
At church on Sundays see no woman dare
Go for communion in front of her –
If they presume to move, so wrath is she,
Goodbye all thoughts of Christian charity! –
And thrice she'd travelled to Jerusalem
Calling at Rome, as she came back again –
To Sant Iago once – at Compostella –
Boulogne, Cologne . . . Why would she want to go to Boulogne?

PARDONER.
Why would anybody want to go to Boulogne, dearheart? Either to visit the shrine of Our Lady, or to pick up a Frenchman.

CHAUCER.
She was an upright woman all her life,
To tell the truth she'd been through husbands five,
Not counting other company in youth –

WIFE.
Five husbands at the Church door – Yes, that's truth.
Why should I be ashamed of quantity?
They all were worthy men to some degree. (*Laughs.*)
I'm looking for the sixth – long, short or tall,
In sooth, I don't like chastity at all.
As soon as one husband's from this world gone
I'm praying for the next to come along,
For then, th'Apostle says that I am free! –
To wed, and bed whoever pleases me.
St Paul has just the text to serve my turn:
'Better,' he says, 'to marry than to burn!'

PRIORESS.
But –

WIFE OF BATH.
Why should I care if folk look down on me?
I know we all must prize virginity –
And continence, and eke devotion too –
But, as for me, I'd rather let it go.
Christ knows we can't all live the perfect life
Perfect's for nuns. I'd rather be a wife.

PRIORESS.
The perfect life can never be, my dear,
And yet it must be sought, and strived after –

WIFE OF BATH.
Tell me one thing, then – to what conclusion
Were organs made for copulation?

PRIORESS.
O –

WIFE OF BATH.
These cunning little things – why were they wrought?
Trust me, my lords, they were not made for nought.
Some say God gave us them for passing water
Some say so we could tell our sons from daughters –
I say such folk have never lived, nor thrived.
Well, I have lived – five husbands I've survived!
Each one of them tried hard to rein me in
But in the end I got the bett'r of him,
And led him by the nose, and had my way,
By cunning, force, or nagging night and day.
O in my bed – that's where the fun was best!
I'd grouche and chide and never let him rest,
And if he slid his hand up my loose gown
I'd jump from bed and leave him on his own.
I'd say:
'What's wrong with you husband? You moan and groan
Do you think my cunny's yours, and yours alone?
Catch as catch can – let's see you do your stuff
St Peter knows you brag of it enough.'
Until, at last, some gift he'd promise me

And then I'd let him 'do his nicetee.'
I tell ye, men, which way this mad world goes:
It's all for sale, but you'll pay through the nose.
Of all the husbands, though, I've held in thrall
I think I loved the fifth the best of all
Like cats and dogs in sacks we fought full sore
He beat me till my ribs were red and raw
I'll bear the scars until the judgement day
But in our bed he was so fresh and gay
He'd whisper words of love and kiss me close
I never could deny him my "belle chose."
And though he often hurt me – did me wrong
He'd win my love again before too long.
O yes! – I loved him best, because, you see
I went in fear that he might not love me.
The truth about us women – I'll not lie
Is that we have a curious fantasy
Where love's denied, or proves too hard to gain,
That love we'll cry all day for and complain.
And shall I tell you why my ear is deaf?
Out of this husband's book I tore a leaf . . . or two.
It was a book that, gladly, night and day
For his enlightenment he'd read alway
Containing all the history and lives
Of all the world's most wickedest of wives.
Upon a night my husband, book in hand,
Sat by the fire to read of womankind:
He read of Eve and all her wickedness
That brought our first father to wretchedness.
He read of Samson and his treacherous wife
Who cut his hair off with her pocket knife
And Socrates who meekly nothing said
When *his* wife tipped a piss-pot on his head,
He read of Parsiphae, the queen of Crete
He thought her tale particularly sweet –
Who cuckolded her husband with a bull –
Enough of that – too much! His book was full
Of all the women Roman, Greek, and Jew
Who brought this world to misery and woe.
And when I saw that he would not give o'er

I grabbed it from him, and three pages tore,
At which he jumped and let out a great shout!
So with my fist I gave him such a clout
That knocked him off his stool into the fire!
How like a lion did he rage and roar
And with clenched fist he punched me in the head
Down on the floor I fell as I were dead.
It was that blow – that blow upon my ear
That made me deaf – I've been so many a year.
O how I loved him! – Words could never tell.
I pray God keep his sweet soul out of hell!
For in the end – in spite of cares and woe
We made it up, and lived in peace, we two.
And so he placed the bridle in my hand
Giving me governance of house and land.
But, Dear Lord Christ, when I remember me
Of all my youth and all my jollity
It tickles me right down to my heart's root!
Unto this day – O it doth mine heart good,
That I have known the world – I've had my time!
Old age envenoms pleasure – it doth mine –
Bereaving me my beauty and my pith.
Well, let it go! The devil go therewith!
My flour is sold – that's all there is to tell –
Now all I'm left with is the chaff to sell.
So God bless husbands, of His mercy dear!
Now will I tell my tale, if you will hear.

FRIAR (*laughing*).
May God, good woman, send you a quick sale!
This was a strange preamble to a tale!

SUMMONER.
What if it was? Who asked you to chime in?
A friar will poke his nose in everything.
They say that flies and friars most buzz around
Wherever food or filth may fall to ground.

FRIAR.
O, say'st thou so, sir Summ'ner? I tell you
Before we part I'll tell a tale or two,
About a summoner, shall make us smile.

SUMMONER.

Beshrew thy face – beshrew me too the while,
If I don't tell a tale or two – or three –
About a friar, before we see the sea
At Sidyngbourne. O, I shall make thee smart!

HOST.

Peace! And that anon! And keep ye apart!
Good woman, start your tale – and do your best.

WIFE OF BATH.

I'm ready, sir, to do so, if ye list,
If I have licence of this worthy friar.

FRIAR.

Yes, Madame, yes. You speak and I will hear.

Thirteen: The Wife of Bath's Tale

WIFE OF BATH.

In th'olden days – the days of King Arthúr
One whom the Britons hold in great honour –
All filled with fairy folk was this our land.
The elf-queen, with her courtiers hand in hand,
Full often danced upon the meads of green,
And oft by human kind would they be seen.
I speak of many hundred years ago.
These days you won't see any elves no moe,
Because of the hard work of priests and friars
Who with their holiness, and endless prayers
Have found their way to every strand and stream
As thick as motes that dance in a sunbeam,
And bless our halls, and chambers, kitchens, bowers,
Our cities, burghs, and castles, and high towers,
Our thorpes, our barns, our shippons, and our dairies.
With Holy Church, who feels the need for fairies?

And so befell it that this King Arthúr
Had in his house a lusty bachelor

Who on a day espied a pretty maid
And by main force bereft her maidenhead,
For which oppression there was such outcry
King Arthur straight condemned the youth to die –
By course of law he should have lost his head –
All ravishers, the law says, must be dead.
But then the Queen, and other ladies moe,
Begged of the King that it might not be so.
And to the Queen King Arthur gave her will –
He gave him her to save or else to spill.
And so she summoned him upon a day:

QUEEN.
Thou standest yet, young man, in such array
That of thy life thou hast no surety.
I'll save thy head, if thou canst say to me
What thing it is that women most desire.
Look that thou keepst thy neck-bone from our ire.

YOUNG KNIGHT.
I . . .

QUEEN.
Well?

YOUNG KNIGHT.
I . . . I can't tell.

QUEEN.
Well . . . since thou cannot answer me anon,
Yet will I give thee leave to get thee gone
To seek and search a twelve-month and a day
And find sufficient answer, if ye may.
And sureties I will have, ere ye go,
Thy body for to yield to wele or woe.

WIFE OF BATH.
What could he do? Nothing – save sigh, and wend
And swear to come again at one year's end.
He asks at every house and every place,
Hoping to find an answer by God's grace:

YOUNG KNIGHT.
What thing is it that women most desire?

WIFE OF BATH.
But he could never find at any price
Two woman who would say the same thing twice.
Some said:

WOMAN 1.
That's easy – we love best richesse.

WOMAN 2.
Nay, that's not so. We best love jollyness.

WOMAN 3.
Nay – rich array –

WOMAN 4.
Nay, nay – it's fun in bed.

WOMAN 5.
To wed a young man, handsome, kind and good.

WOMAN 6.
Most married women pray for widowhood.

WOMAN 7.
I know the answer, sir, I will not lie,
The thing a maid loves best is flattery.

WOMAN 8.
I'll tell you what the thing I think most nice is:
It's when a man pretends we have no vices.

YOUNG KNIGHT.
How can man know what woman loveth so?

WIFE OF BATH.
The day approached when he must homeward go,
And in his way it happened he must ride,
In all his wretchedness, by forest's side
Where in a glade he saw by strangest chance
'Bove four-and-twenty ladies in a dance,
Closer he crept, but e'en as he drew near
Vanished was the dance, he knew not where.
No creature could he find – they all had gone –
Save on the green he saw an ancient crone –
A fouler wight there may no man devise –

As he approached her, she began to rise,
And said:

CRONE.
Sir knight, here lieth not your way.
Tell me what thing you seek, upon your fey!
I may, and peradventure, end your woe.
We wise old women see more than you know.

YOUNG KNIGHT.
My dear old mother, one thing I know well
I am but dead tomorrow. I can't tell
What thing it is that women most desire!
Could you assist me, I'd pay well your hire.

CRONE.
Plight me thy truth – here give your hand to me –
Swear the next thing that I require of thee
Thou shalt fulfil, if it lie in thy might,
And I'll resolve your riddle ere't be night.

YOUNG KNIGHT.
Have here my truth! All that you ask I grant!

CRONE.
Then I dare swear to you, my young gallant,
Thy life is saved. I stand by what I say
The Queen will pardon you – she'll not say nay.
Set me before the proudest of them all,
Dressed in their jewelled finery withal,
None will deny the answer I shall teach.
Let us go forth withouten further speech.

WIFE OF BATH.
When they were come into the court, this knight
Said he had kept his day, and done them right.

YOUNG KNIGHT.
I have my answer ready, 'pon my life.

WIFE OF BATH.
Came many a maid, and many a noble wife,
Came many a widow, wise, shrewd, and discreet.
The Queen herself approached the judgement seat

And all her court his answer came to hear.
The young man had his summons to appear –

QUEEN.
Silence! To every wyght I bid silence!
And now, sir knight, say to this audience:
What thing it is that women most desire?

YOUNG KNIGHT.
I'll answer, Majesty, as you require:
The thing all women want is sovereignty
O'er their husbands. That same servility,
Shown by a lover to his fair lady,
They want from husbands. Complete mastery.
This is your chief desire, though you me kill.
Do as you list. I'm subject to your will.

QUEEN.
Well. Well. Well . . .

WIFE OF BATH.
In all that court no widow, wife, nor maid
Could contradict the thing the knight had said.

QUEEN.
Your life, I judge, you have worthily won.

WIFE OF BATH.
And at her words up starts the ancient crone –
The one had taught the knight what he should say:

CRONE.
O let me speak my sovereign, if I may!
Ere that your court depart, pray do me right.
I taught this subtle answer to yon knight,
For which he hath plighted me his truth there
The first thing of him that I would require,
He'd do it if it lay within his might.
Before this court, I pray of you, sir knight,
That thou will take me here unto thy wife –
For well thou know'st how I have saved your life.
I speak the truth. Thou cans't not say me nay.

YOUNG KNIGHT.
Alas, old crone! Alas and weylawey!
I know it well that such was my behest –
But for God's love! – choose some other request!
Take all my goods, and let my body go.

CRONE.
And if I do, may God curse both us two!
Though I be foul, and wrinkled, old and poor,
I will not for the gold, nor yet the ore
That in the earth is graved, nor lieth above,
Have aught but thy fair body – and thy love!

YOUNG KNIGHT.
My love! My love! Nay – my damnatiön!
Alas a knight so young – of such high station –
Should by one foul and old disparaged be!

WIFE OF BATH.
'Twas all for nought. The end was this: that he
Constreynéd was. They said that he must wed
His foul old crone – and take her to his bed.
The nuptials passed in heaviness and sorrow
And privily they married on the morrow.
And all that day he hid him like an owl
So woe he was to wed a wife so foul.
But greater was his woe – his heart like lead –
When he was forced to take her into bed.

CRONE.
My husband, dear! Ah, benedicitee
Is every young knight blithe in bed as ye?
Is this how things are in King Arthur's house?
Are all his young men quite so timorous?
O am I not your bride – your love – your wife?
Am I not she who rescued your young life?
And, certes, have I done you no unright –
Why fare ye thus with me on our first night?
Ye faren like a man hath lost his will.
What is my guilt? If I have done thee ill
Say how, and I'll amend it if I may.

YOUNG KNIGHT.

Amend it! How? Amend it? Nay, nay, nay!
It will not be amended – nevermoe.
Thou art so ugly, and so foul also –
Of lowly stock – so old and so infirm –
Is't any wonder that I faint and squirm?
I would to God my beating heart would burst!

CRONE.

Is it only this? – the cause of your unrest?

YOUNG KNIGHT.

'Only' she says! Can you wonder at it!

CRONE.

And mend it too – if you'd use a little wit.
You set such store by your gentility
Old wealth amassed by old nobility –
You seem to think that makes a gentle man?
Such arrogance abandon if you can
And learn that true gentility is born
Of virtuous deeds – intended and performed.
Who always does what gentle deeds he can
Him do I judge the greatest gentleman.
Christ wills of Him we claim our gentleness
Not from our ancestors, nor their richesse.
For though they leave us all their heritage
They cannot leave the wisdom of their age
Nor yet their honour nor their chivalry.
A youth must earn respect through courtesy –
It is his own! – acquired through virtuous living.
In this his ancestry amounts to nothing.
Nor is gentility a thing for show –
To be put off when men are on their own.
Take fire, and bear it to the darkest house
At the world's end – the furthest Caucuses –
And let men shut the doors and go therefrom
Yet will that fire flame up and brightly burn,
As warm as twenty thousand looked thereon.
Good deeds will make a youth into a man.
And wicked deeds will make a youth a churl –

Yea! – though his father were a Duke or Earl.
And therefore my dear husband I conclude,
All be it though my ancestors were rude,
God grant me to live ever free from sin
Then am I gentle. Honour doth begin
With me – I own and claim it, and it's mine! –
New minted, bright – not old and dull like thine.
Then you reproved me for my poverty,
My lowliness, and meek humility.
I say, sir, poverty's an honest thing –
And I have heard, My Lord, who's heaven's King
Chose poverty when He came down to earth.
Poverty, full oft – when man is of low birth –
Brings him to God, and makes him know himself.
And therefore, sir, I say – for all your wealth –
Do not look down on poverty in me.
You call me foul and old – that's what you said –
Then thank the Lord you won't be cuckolded!
For filthiness and age – I can tell ye –
Are great custodians of chastity.
But nonetheless, since I know your delight,
I shall fulfil your carnal appetite.
Now you must choose. Choose well, and choose for aye:
To have me foul and old until I die,
And yet to be your true, and humble wife,
And never to displease you all my life.
Or – if you will – to have me young and fair.
And risk the lust of rivals – as ye dare.

YOUNG KNIGHT.
My lady, and my love, my wife and dear,
I place myself in your wise governance.
Choose for yourself, for I will take my chance,
Do what you think will bring us most honour.
Which it may be I neither know nor care
For as you like, so it sufficeth me.

CRONE.
Then in my hands you place your mastery?
Since I may choose and govern as I list?

YOUNG KNIGHT.
You may, my wife. Whatever you think best.

CRONE.
Kiss me, fair sir, and be no longer wrothe,
For here, I swear, I will to you be both –
That is to say to ye – both fair and good.
I pray to God that I may run stark mad
If I am ever faithless and untrue.
I'll prove the faithfullest since th'world was new.
And but I be at morn as fair beseen
As any lady, empëress, or queen,
That ever lived betwixt the east and west,
Grant me my life or death as you think best.
Pull back the curtain. See me as I am.

YOUNG KNIGHT.
Now, by my faith, I am once more a man!

WIFE OF BATH.
O she was fair and sweet, and young thereto!
For joy he clasped her in his armës two –
His heart was bathëd in a bath of bliss –
A thousand times, and more, he gan her kiss,
And she obeyed his will in everything
All was for his pleasure and his liking.
And thus they lived and loved till their lives' end,
In perfect joy! And Jesus Christ us send
Husbands as young, and meek, and fresh in bed,
And grace to overmaster those we wed.
And eek I pray to Jesus: stint their lives
That will not be the playthings of their wives!

Applause, laughter, etc.

FRIAR.
May God, my dame, give you a right good life!
This was a wondrous way to win a wife.
Now, if it liketh all our company
I have a tale that I would tell to ye
About a summoner – a tale of villainy.
All summoners – ye know – do knavery –

Of the whole pack, what good was ever known?
Summ'ners are rogues who run about the town
Arresting folk who will not bribe them well,
But keep from court those thieves who'll share their spoil.
Summoners are scum – they all deserve a beating!

CHAUCER.
Now steady, sir! Such language is not fitting.
On with your tale, and let our Summoner be.

SUMMONER.
Nay, spare ye not! And let him say of me
What so him list. My turn will come right soon.
By God, I shall be quits with him anon.
I'll show you all what flatterers are these friars,
What greedy graspers, lechers, cheats, and liars –

HOST.
Now hold thy peace! Let's have no more of this.
Tell forth your tale, sir, and 'tis time ywis.

Fourteen: The Friar's Tale

FRIAR.
Whilom there was, dwelling in my country,
An Archdeacon, a man of high degree,
Who in the Bishop's court punished those crimes
Which have so multiplied in these sad times,
As witchcraft, brothelcraft, idolatry
As defamation, and adultery,
As church reves, and as false-sworn testaments,
As contracts broke, and lack of sacraments,
As usury, and simony also –
To lechers, though, he dealt the greatest woe:
If they came into court for such a thing
He'd lash them with his tongue and make them sting.
For ere the Bishop caught them with his crook
Their sins were inked in this Archdeacon's book.

He had a summ'nor ready and on hand
The slyest boy in all of Engerland
Who used a subtle web of paid informers
To whisper him where lechery was warmest –
For he would spare of lechers one or two
To lead the way to four-and-twenty moe.
Then had he placed his bawds down in the stews
Who kept him well supplied with all the news –
They told him all men's secrets privily.
He took himself a great profit thereby –
His master, the Archdeacon, never guessed
How richly this lewd man had lined his nest.
He'd serve some forged court summons on a sinner
And they would fill his purse, or buy his dinner –
Then he would say:

SUMMONER 2.
My friend, now for thy sake,
I'll tear this summons with its letters black.
Thou shalt namore in this hard case travail –
I am thy friend, when I may thee avail.

FRIAR.
In all this world, no hound could trace a scent
As could this summoner, in search of rent.
It so befell that once upon a day
Our summ'nor rode abroad seeking his prey
He'd forged a summons for some widow poor,
Feigning a case to force a bribe from her,
And as it happ'd he saw before him ride
A yeoman gay, out of a woody glade.
A bow he bore, and arrows bright and keen
He wore a jerkin like the forest green –
A hat upon his head with feathers black.

SUMMONER 2.
Hail and well met, sir! Will you turn your back?

DEVIL.
What would'stow, man? Would'st ride along with me?

SUMMONER 2.
Where rydestow? I'll join ye if I may.

DEVIL.
Be welcome then. Is't far ye ride today?

SUMMONER 2.
Nay, here fast by. 'Tis but a little way.
For, saying soothly, it is mine intent
To ride a while and raise a little rent.
Unto my lord the payment's fallen due.

DEVIL.
O you're a bailiff then? Well I'm one too.

SUMMONER 2.
Why, yes I am!

FRIAR.
He daren't confess for shame
That he's a summoner! O filthy name!

SUMMONER.
You may, you may! My turn will come anon.

FRIAR.
A filthy name, I say –

HOST.
Sir, peace! Get on!

DEVIL.
I am a stranger, sir, in this country.
Of thine acquaintance then I would pray thee –
Brotherhood too – we'll share all if you list.
You shall draw gold and silver from my chest
If that you hap to come into our shire –
All shall be thine – all as thou would desire.

SUMMONER 2.
Grantmercy, sir! A bargain by my faith!
And thou shalt share in everything I have!
Now brother, where d'you dwell? – I prithee say –
For certain, I shall visit you someday.

DEVIL.
My dwelling, brother? Far i'th' North country.
And there, I hope, some time I shall thee see.

SUMMONER 2.

Then since we're new sworn brothers, as you say,
Pray teach me, while we're riding by the way,
Since you're a debt collector as am I,
Some of your subtle tricks. Tell faithfully
How to abuse our office, gold to win.
Leave nothing out for conscience' sake nor sin,
But as a brother tell me all you do.

DEVIL.

Now, by my truth, my brother – since you'd know –
I'll tell thee faithfully my sorry tale:
My living is but strait, my wages small;
My lord to me is hard and dangerous
Mine office is to me laborious
And, therefore, by extortion I must live.
For sooth, I take whatever men will give.
Always by cunning or by violence
From year to year I win all my dispence.
For, by my faith, I know no other way.

SUMMONER 2.

Now certés, brother, certés – so fare I!
I care not what I steal, now God it wot,
Unless it be too heavy or too hot.
What I may get by secret conveyance
I take – and devil take my conscience!
Without extortion I could not live –
Nor will I take my soul to church to shrive.
Stomach no conscience, confess to none –
And curse father-confessors – every one!
Well are we met, by God and by Saint James!
But, lever brother, tell me now your name.

DEVIL.

Brother, pause there. My name you'd have me tell?
I am a fiend. My dwelling is in hell.
And here I ride about my purchasing
To know what men will give me anything.
Men's gifts make up the most part of my rent.
And here thou ridest with the same intent –
To win great wealth – thou carest never how,

No more than I – for I would ride from now
Unto the world's end, only to get my prey . . .

SUMMONER 2.
Ah, benedicite! What's that ye say?
Ye have a manly shape as well as I –
I thought ye were a yeoman – truthfully.
Have ye a figure then determinate
When you're in hell, and lord in your estate?

DEVIL.
Nay, certainly, in hell, we have no form,
But when it liketh us we can take one,
Or make it seem to you we have a shape –
Sometimes we go like men, sometimes an ape,
Or like an angel can I ride or go.
It's no great wonder, though you think it so.
A lousy juggler fooleth such as thee,
And, God he knows, I ken more craft than he.

SUMMONER 2.
Why change your shape at all? Why not just one?

DEVIL.
With several shapes each several prey is won.

SUMMONER 2.
It seems to me you give yourself much labour.

DEVIL.
I do. Would'st thou know why, my lever neighbour?
Sometimes we fiends must be God's instruments –
A means to do his high commandëments,
When that He list, upon His creätures,
In divers arts, employing diverse figures.
Our power is weak unless God sanctions it;
If he opposes, then we must submit.
But sometime, if we ask, we're given leave
Only the body, not the soul, to grieve –
Witness on Job to whom we did much woe.
Sometimes we're sent to wrestle with men's souls
For when a man withstands temptation
It is great cause of his salvation.

Not that we hope the struggle turns out well,
We try our best to drag his soul to hell.

SUMMONER 2.
Yet tell me, faithfully, D'ye make alway
New bodies from the elements?

DEVIL.
Nay! Nay.
Sometimes we cast delusions 'fore your eyes,
At other times we make dead bodies rise
And speak as cunningly and well
As did the witch who raised up Samuel.
But let me warn thee now – I do not jape –
One day you'll learn how fiends can change their shape.
Nor shalt thou need my help, my brother dear;
Experience will teach thee – never fear!
Now ride we on, for I will stay with thee,
Unless it be that thou forsakest me.

SUMMONER 2.
What! Leave ye? Nay! That never shall betide
I never break my word – it's known full wide –
For though thou were't that fallen Lucifer
I never would forsake my brother here.
Seize what you can – whatever men will give
And I shall too – and this is how we'll thrive.
And if that either one wins more than th'other
Let him be true, and share it with his brother.

DEVIL.
I grant it ye, my brother, by my fey.

FRIAR.
So summoner and devil went their way,
And as they reached the gate at the town's end
Through which they both were shaping for to wend
They saw a cart full loaded up with hay
Slide back and forth, and lie across their way,
Deep in the ruts and stuck fast in the mud.
The carter smote his horses like one wood:

CARTER.
Hey, Brok! Hay, Scot! Why slip ye on the stones?

The devil fetch'ee, body, hooves, and bones!
For all these woes you bring me, new and old,
I curse the day as ever ye were foaled!
Devil take all – my horses, cart and hay!

SUMMONER 2.
Did you hear that? Now shall we have some play!
Hearken, my brother – hearken by thy faith –
Herestow not there what that carter saith?
Take it at once, for he hath give it thee –
His cart, his hay, and eek his horses three.

DEVIL.
Nay, brother, nay! Believe it never a del.
For he meant nothing by it – trust me well –
Ask him yourself, if thou wilt not trust me,
Or stint a while and see what thou shalt see.

FRIAR.
This carter thwacked his horses on the croup
And they began to drawen out and stoop.

CARTER.
Hey, now! Well done! There! Jesus Christ you bless
And all His toiling creatures, more and less!
That was well pulled, my sweet, mine own grey boy!
I pray God save thee all – Ah, by Saint Loy!
Now is my cart out of the slough, Perdee!

DEVIL.
Lo, brother! Did'st thou mark what I told thee?
Herein may you see, mine own dear brother,
The churl spake one thing, but he thought another.
Let us go forth and search out other gains
Here will I win but little for my pains.

SUMMONER 2.
Brother, watch me. Here lives a poor old wreck
Who would almost as lief as break her neck,
As for to lose a penny that she had.
I'll get twelve pence off her, though she be mad,
Or I will summonse her unto our court.
And yet, God knows I know, she hath done nought –

She hath no vice in her. But thou shalt see
How well we manage things in this country.

He beats on the door.

Come down! Come out! Thou sely muttonhead!
I trow thou hast some friar in thy bed,
Or else a priest or two –

OLD WIFE.
Who clappeth there?

SUMMONER 2.
'Tis I, th'Archdeacon's man! Now get down here!

OLD WIFE.
God save you, sir. I pray you, what's your will?

SUMMONER 2.
I have a summons here – writ in this bill.
On pain of cursing – look here – thou must be
Tomorrow morn before th'Archdeacon's knee
To answer in his court of certain things.

OLD WIFE.
Now Lord, Christ Jesu save us! King of Kings,
Have mercy on me! Save me if you may!
I have been sickly, and for many a day –
I may not walk so far! I cannot ride –
The pain would be my death – here, in my side.
What's my offence? And who accuseth me?
May I not send my answer, sir, by thee?

SUMMONER 2.
Yes, that ye may, if ye will pay – let's see –
Twelve pence? – yes, twelve – then I can set you free.
My master gets it all. It's him you pay.
Come on, come on! I must be on my way.

OLD WIFE.
Saint Mary help me out of care and sin!
If all the world were there for me to win
I could not find twelve pence to have and hold.
Have pity, sir, you see that I am old –
Show charity unto a poor, weak wretch.

SUMMONER 2.
Nay then, old sot, may the foul fiend me fetch
If I excuse thee, though thy life be spilt –

OLD WIFE.
Alas! Alas! God knows, I have no guilt –

SUMMONER 2.
Pay me! Come on! And by the sweet Saint Anne,
I'll take with me that bright new copper pan
For payment of a debt thou owe'st of old –
Come give it me, old witch. Let go thy hold!

OLD WIFE.
Old witch! What debt? I never had no debt –

SUMMONER.
For cuckolding your man – thou owe'st me yet.
I paid at court for your correction –

OLD WIFE.
Thou liar, thou! By my salvation
Never ere now, as widow nor as wife
Was I in court! – not once in all my life!
Nor never was but of my body true!
Unto the foulest fiend of blackest hue
I'll give my pan, before I give it you.

DEVIL.
Now Mabel, dear old mother, by your fey,
Is this your will, in earnest, that ye say?

OLD WIFE.
The devil fetch his soul – 'Twas my intent –
And pan and all, unless he will repent.

SUMMONER 2.
Repent! Old stoat! I will not pardon thee
Of any penny that thou owe'st to me!

DEVIL *collars him.*

DEVIL.
Thy body and this pan are mine by right.
Thou shalt with me to hell this very night,

Where thou shalt learn, more of our faculty
Than any Doctor of Divinity.

They fly to Hell.

FRIAR.
And with that word this foul fiend hath him hente.
Body and soul he with the devil went,
To where all summoners are lodged in hell –

SUMMONER.
And where are friars kept? Now will I tell?
This friar boasts he knows his way about
The fiery pit. It's true – I've little doubt –
And God He knows that it is little wonder! –
Friars and fiends are never long asunder.
Lordings, pardee, have ye not heard it tell
How that a friar was carried off to hell?
An angel showed him all the torments there –
But in that place he never saw a friar.
All other folk he saw them writhe in woe.
Unto this angel spoke the friar so:
'Good sir,' quoth he, 'are friars in such grace
That none of them shall come into this place?'
'Nay!' saith the angel. 'We have millions here.'
And led him down where Satan hath his lair.
'You see,' he said, 'that Satan hath a tail
Broader, and wider than a carrack's sail.
Satan, hold up thy tail! Obey!' quoth he,
'Show forth thine arse, and let this friar see
Where stands the friars' convent in this place!'
The tail rose up a furlong into space
And just like bees that swarm out from a hive,
All farted from his arse did Satan drive
Full twenty thousand friars in a rout,
And through all hell those friars were blown about,
Then flit for home, for Satan's shitten bum,
And up his arse they scrambled every one.
(*To the* FRIAR.) That's the eternal dwelling of your kind,
So keep the devil's arse, sir, in your mind.
God save us all! – except this filthy friar,
I will not waste more words on such a liar.

FRIAR.
Right! That's it –

Then a fight – a sort of clerical scrum – the PARDONER *joins in on the* SUMMONER*'s side, beating the* FRIAR *about the head with a large thurible.*

CHAUCER.
Part them! They are incensed!

End of Part Three.

Interval.

PART FOUR

Fifteen: The Clerk of Oxenford's Tale

CLERK.

There is, upon Italia's western strand,
Around the foot of Vesulus the cold,
A fertile plain, abundant fruitful land,
Where many a tower and town thou mayst behold
That founded were in Roman times of old,
With many another captivating sight,
And Saluces this noble region hight.

A marquis whilom lord was of that land,
As were his worthy ancestors before,
And obeisant, and ready to his hand,
Were all his liegemen – all, both less and more.
Thus in delight he lived, through days of yore.
Through Fortune's favour he was feared and loved,
Both lords and people his good rule approved.
Save for one thing:

FIRST LORD.

O noble marquis, your humanity
Assureth us, and gives us hardiness
To speak out in our great necessity,
To voice our sorrow and our heaviness.
Accept it, Lord, now of your gentillesse,
That we with piteous hearts to you complain,
And let your ears our voices ne'er distain.

SECOND LORD.

For, certes, Lord, so well we loveth you
And all your good works – so much so that we
Could scarce imagine when, or where, or how
A people could wish more felicity –
Save for one thing . . . Lord, if your will it be
To be a wedded man – as ye think best –
Then would your people think them truly blessed.

FIRST LORD.

O bow your neck under that blissful yoke!
'Tis sovereign service, not a servitude.
Wedlock's the best – the sweetest sort of lock –
Bethink yourself of that beatitude
For Time doth filch our days with fingers rude,
And though we sleep, or wake, or roam or ride,
Time stealeth on – He will no man abide.

OLD LORD.

Think, though your green of youth's in flower yet,
Age creepeth on – though seeming still as stone –
Death threatens old – and young – his spear will smite
At all estates, for there escapeth none,
Except that in his children he lives on.
Protect your heritage – keep hope alive!
Provide us with an heir! For God's sake, wive!

WALTER (*pronounced 'Water'*).

Well . . . Well . . . I've giv'n no thought, ere now, to wives,
For I rejoice in liberty much more,
But here I charge you all – upon your lives –
If I should take a wife ye'll me assure
To honour her, while that her life endure,
In word and deed, at court and everywhere,
As she the daughter of an emperor were.

And, furthermore, this shall ye swear: that ye
Against my choice shall never grudge nor strive.
For, since I must forgo my liberty
At your request, as ever I may thrive,
Where as my heart is set, there will I wive.
And but ye give assent to what I wish,
I pray you, let me hear no more of this.

CLERK.

With heartiest will they swear and they assent
To all he asked – no man would say him nay,
And straightway he declared 'twas his intent
To bid a feast against his wedding day,
And all his knights and squires their lord obey,
And each of them does all his diligence

To show unto the feast great reverence.
The day of wedding's come, but no one can
Tell who their Lord's intended bride should be,
For which strange marvel wondered many a man
And murmured when they were in privacy:

FIRST LORD.
I fear our Lord won't leave his vanity.

SECOND LORD.
Will he not wed? Alas, alas the while!

OLD LORD.
Why doth he thus himself and us beguile?

CLERK.
This royal marquis in his best array
With lords and ladies in his company –
All bidden to his wedding feast that day –
And with his retinue of bachelory,
With many a merry sound of melody
Rode out towards a village that he knew.
And not a soul could guess what he would do.

MAIDEN 1.
Grisilde! Grisilde!

MAIDEN 2.
Come down, Grisilde!

GRISILDE.
I will with all the other maidens stand
To see the marquis and his bride pass by.

MAIDEN 1.
Step up here, Grisilde.

MAIDEN 2.
Give me your hand.

GRISILDE.
I must go back as soon as it may be.

WALTER.
Grisilde? Where's your father, Grisilde?
Go in, at once, and fetch him out to me.

GRISILDE *brings her old* FATHER *out of the cottage,* WALTER *takes him aside.*

Janicula, I neither may, nor can
No longer bear, what's in my heart to hide –
There is no need to tremble thus, good man!
If thou vouchsafe, whatever may betide,
Whatever others say on either side,
Thy daughter will I take unto my wife,
And love her to the ending of my life.

JANICULA.
Mother of God!

WALTER.
And here and now I beg thee and implore
That you'll accept me as your son-in-law.

JANICULA.
What can I answer, Lord? My heart is yours
What e'er your will is, so is mine perforce.

WALTER.
Grisild. Come here. Ye well shall understand,
It's pleasing to your father and to me
That I wed you – that you give me your hand.
If you consent to wed, so let it be.
I am in haste, and may make no long stay.
Will ye assent? Come, speak – what do ye say?

JANICULA.
Daughter? This is your lord –

WALTER.
Further I say, be ready with good heart
To do my will as freely as ye may,
As I think best, whether ye laugh or smart,
And ne'er to grudge it, not by night nor day.
When I say 'yes' you must not answer 'nay' –
Neither by word, nor frowning countenance –
Swear this, and here I swear our alliance.

JANICULA.
Answer, child.

GRISILDE.

Lord, I am poor and unworthy
Of these great dignities you offer me
But as you will yourself, right so will I,
And here I swear that never knowingly
In deed, nor thought, your will I'll disobey –
Not for my life – though I'd be loath to die –

WALTER.

Enough – this is enough, Grisilde mine.

LADIES *remove every stitch of* GRISILDE*'s clothes and dress her in rich bridal garments.* WALTER *presents her with rich jewels, and weds her with a ring in front of his* BISHOP.

This is my wife. Before ye she stands here.
Show her all honour. Love her too, I pray,
All ye who love me. There's namore to say.

CLERK.

Thus Walter lowly – nay, right royally –
Wedded with Fortune and with honesty,
In God's fair peace liveth full easily
At home, and outward grace enough had he.
For he had seen that under low degree
Virtue is often hid. And so the people held him
A good and prudent man, as they do seldom.

Not only this. Grisilde through her wit
Knew everything of wifely homeliness
But also, when the State had need of it
All public disagreements could redress.
There was no discord, rancour, heaviness,
In all the land that she could not appease
And wisely bring them all to calm and ease.

In course of time Grisild a daughter bore,
And though she would have rather born a boy,
Glad was this marquis and his folk therefore –
Her husband's love for her grew more and more,
And yet he wished to test her constancy –
Needless, God knows, such callous cruelty.

WALTER.
Grisilde?
Ye wot yourself how I have brought you here
Into my house – it is not long ago –
And though to me you are most lief and dear,
Unto my nobles ye be nothing so.
They say, to them it is great shame and woe
That all their high estate should bow so low –
To one whose father walked behind a plough.

GRISILDE.
What would you have me do?

WALTER.
Nothing.
I must do with thy daughter for the best –
Not as I'd wish, but as my people list.
And yet, God knows, it is full loath to me . . .
But none the less, if it's without your blessing,
I will not do it. Say – what shall it be?
Do you assent to me in such a thing?
Show me the patience and devotion
That once ye swore to me back in your village
The day I came and asked your hand in marriage.

GRISILDE.
Husband and lord, all lies in your pleasing.
My child and I with heart felt obeisance
Are both your own. And you must save or spill
What is your own. I pray you, do your will.

Nothing that pleases you, so God me save,
Displeases me, nor e'er shall displease me.
And there is nothing I desire to have,
Nor fear to lose, but saving only thee.
These words come from my heart as you can see.
No length of time, nor death may this deface,
Nor change my heart, nor yet my love displace.

WALTER.
I am glad of it.

Exit.

SERGEANT.

Madame, I beg, ye will forgive it me,
Though I do things to which I am constrained.
You are so wise, and it is known to thee
That lord's commands must not be slacked, nor blamed –
Though they may be bewailed, cursed and complained.
A man must needs his master's will obey
And so must I . . . There is namore to say.
This child I am commanded for to take.

GRISILDE.

Hold off a while. Be patient for my sake.
Farewell, my child! I shall thee no more see
But since that I have signed thee with the cross,
Of Christ, thy father – may he blessed be! –
That died for us upon the cruel tree,
I pray this night He will thy soul betake,
For you must die, my child, and for my sake.

Go quickly now, and do my lord's behest,
But one thing will I beg thee of thy grace
That, but my lord forbid it, you at least
Bury this little body in some place
That beasts and birds may do it no disgrace.

CLERK.

The sergeant goes, and hath fulfilled this thing.
But to the marquis straight return must we,
Who falls to contemplation – wondering
If in his wife's demeanour he might see,
Or by reproachful words, perceive that she
Were changed. But he in her could nothing find
That was not faithful, gentle, true and kind.
In this estate there passed four happy year,
Ere she gave birth again. Then, as God willed,
A baby boy she bore to Lord Walter
Full fair of face and gracious to behold.
And when the news was to the marquis told,
Not only he – the whole country rejoiced,
And thanked God for the child, all with one voice.
But when the boy was just gone two years old:

WALTER.

My wife, I know that you have heard ere this,
How people speak against our marriäge,
And more so now since my successor is
Come of so low a birth. In all our age
There never was such discontent at large.
Their murmuring doth make mine ears so smart,
That it well nigh hath broken my poor heart.

Now speak they thus: 'When Lord Walter is gone
Then shall the blood of Janicle succeed,
And be our Lord – for other have we none.'

I'd live in peace with them an if I might.
Wherefore I'm minded, and that suddenly,
As I his sister took from you one night
To take also her brother privily.
I warn you, lest that you would wilfully
Distract yourself. Let no outrage betray
A loss of patience. Blame me not, I pray.

GRISILDE.

I have, My Lord, said thus, and ever shall:
I wish for nothing, wish no thing undone,
But as you wish. I must not grieve at all
Though that my daughter's slain, and now my son,
At your command, if you would have it done.
I have had no part of my children twain,
But sickness first, and after woe and pain.

You are our lord, to do with everything
Right as you list – ask no counsel of me.
For as I left at home mine own clothing,
When first you raised me up from low degree,
I left my will and all my liberty
And took your clothing. Wherefore now I pray
Do all your pleasure – yet will I obey.
And if I thought my death would do you ease,
Right gladly would I die, should it you please.

Kisses her SON *and hands him over to the* SERGEANT.

WALTER (*aside*).

Well do I know that next myself, certain,
She loved her children best in every wise,
And here I ask myself what do I gain,
If these assays of faith will not suffice?
What could a careful husband more devise
To prove her wifehood and her steadfastness?

CLERK.

Yet he continued in his stubbornness.
For which, whereas his people heretofore
Had loved him well, the slander of his shame
Made them to hate where they had loved before.
To be called murd'rer is a hateful name.
But none the less, in earnest – 'twas no game –
He of his cruel purpose would not stint.
To test his wife remained his hidd'n intent.

Ten years went by. One day he called his page.

WALTER.

Write to the Court of Rome in subtle wise –
Inform them of my will with this message:
I'd have them now such breves and bulls devise
As to my secret purpose may suffice,
And say the Pope, all for my peoples' rest,
Bids me to wed another if I list.
And now go fetch my wife.

Certes, Grisild, I had enough pleasence
To take you for my wife, for your goodness,
And for your truth, and for your obeisance
Nought for your lineage, nor great richesse.
But I have learned, in very soothfastness,
'That in great lordship,' so the proverb says,
'There is great servitude in many ways.'

I may not do as every ploughman may.
My people would constrain me for to take
Another wife. They clamour night and day
And now the Pope, their rancour for to slake,
Will give consent – so much I undertake.

The truth is this, my love, I have to say:
My second wife's already on her way.
Be strong of heart, and void at once her place,
And all the dower that ye brought to me
Take it again. I grant it of my grace.
Return again unto your father's house.

GRISILDE.
Husband. My Lord, I know and sense always
How that betwixt your true magnificence
And my poor self, no wight would dare, nor may
Make a comparison. Who'd say me nay?
I never held me worthy in no manner
To be your wife, no not your chamberer.

And in this house, where you made me a lady –
Now God in heaven I take for my witness
He that hath guided me, He that made me –
I held me neither lady, nor its mistress,
But humble servant to your worthiness.
And ever shall, while that my life endure,
Love you – above all worldly creäture.

That ye so long of your gentility
Hath holden me in honour and so nobly
Where as I was not worthy so to be
I thank my God. And now to you I pray:
Take it all back. There is namore to say.
Unto my father gladly will I wend
And with him dwell, until my life shall end.

My Lord, ye know, that in my father's place
Ye did me strip out of my poör weeds
And richly did ye dress me, of your grace.
To you I brought nought else – nothing indeed
But faith, and nakedness, and maidenhead.
And here again your clothing I restore –
And here, your wedding ring, for evermore.
The remnant of your jewels ready be
Within your chamber, safely I dare sayn
Naked I left my father's house for thee
Naked I must go back to him again.
And all your pleasure would I do full fain.

I hope you will not send me on my way
Without a smock to save my modesty.

WALTER.

That smock thou wearest now upon thy back,
Keep it so still. Bear it away with thee.

CLERK.

But hardly could he bear the words to speak,
And hastes away, in tears and for pity.
Before the weeping court herself stripped she,
And in her smock, with head and foot all bare
Towards her father's house forth must she fare.

From Bologna a mighty Earl is come
News of his coming spreads to more and less
And to the poor folk's eärs, all and some,
That he had brought with him a marchioness
As their lord's bride, in pomp and great richesse
Such as was never seen by no man's eye
Throughout the noble land of Lombardy.

The marquis, who had planned and knew all this,
Ere that the Earl was come, sent a message
To summon back poor, simple, Grisildis
And she, with humble heart and glad visage,
Yet with no swelling hopes in her corage,
Came at his hest, and on her knees she fell,
Asked reverently and wisely:

GRISILDE.

What's your will?

WALTER.

Grisilde, I'll speak my mind and openly:
This maiden that shall wedded be to me
Must be received tomorr'w as royally
As in my house it's possible to be.
And also every wight in his degree
Must have his state, in service and in sitting –
All must be done as to mine honour's fitting.

I have no woman equal to the task –
My chambers for t'array in ordinance

As I would wish. And therefore I must ask
That you take all of this in governance.
Thou know'st so well, of old, all my pleasance.
And though thy clothes are rags and somewhat torn
I know thy former skills won't let me down.

GRISILDE.
Not only, lord, as I am glad for thee,
I'll do your will, but I desire also
To serve as best fits my ability
In whatsoever work you'd have me do.
Nor shall I fail, in happiness or woe,
Nor shall the spirit in my heart repent
The love of you – until my life be spent.

Music. GRISILDE *organises the maids and pages in the decoration of the chambers for the wedding feast. Then* WALTER *enters in his wedding robes. Then the* EARL *brings in the sixteen-year-old* BRIDE, *and her twelve-year-old* BROTHER. *Walter's* LORDS, LADIES, *and* PAGES *welcome her.*

FIRST LORD.
Lord Walter is no fool.

SECOND LORD.
She is so fair.

FIRST LADY.
And younger than Grisilde – younger far.

OLD LORD.
The fruit they graft between them will be sweet
And all the nobler from such lineage.

FIRST LORD.
How fair her brother is of his visage.

PAGE.
You said our marquis was a murderer.

FIRST LORD.
Never repeat what hath been said afore,
Now that all turns out well. Prospects are fair –
Our Lord will have a wife, our State an heir.

WALTER (*aside*).
O stormy people, fickle and untrue!
Ay, undiscreet – blown like a weather vane
Delighting most in anything that's new,
Unconstant as the moon ye wax and wane!
Your loud applause all wise men should disdain –
All judgment's false, your constance evil proves.
The man's a fool who trusteth in your loves.

EARL (*to a* LADY).
Tell, if you can – I wonder who is she
That standeth there – dressed in her poverty?

She tells him.

WALTER.
Grisild, come here. Now tell me – what d'you say –
How like ye my new wife and her beauty?

GRISILDE.
Truly, My Lord, right well. For, by my fey,
I never saw a fairer maid than she.
I pray God send her all prosperity –
And to you both I hope that He will send
Pleasance enough unto your lives shall end.

One thing I beg of you – and warn also –
You won't torment too much, nor sharply test
This tender maiden – as you're wont to do –
For she's brought up in such great gentleness,
And was not born to bear unkindliness.
She could not such adversity endure
As could a poor and lowly creäture.

WALTER.
Enough. Grisilde mine – pay heed to me:
Be now no more aghast – no more dismayed.
I have thy faith and all thy constancy,
As well as ever woman was, assayed,
Both in richesse, and poverty arrayed.
And I have found, dear wife, thy steadfastness.

CLERK.
And in his arms he took her and gan kiss.

And she, for wonder of it, took no keep.
The meaning of his words she could not take –
She fared as if she'd started from long sleep
Till from her mazedness she gan awake.

WALTER.
Grisild, I swear, by God that did us make,
Thou art my wife, no other do I have,
Nor never will, as God my soul may save.
This is thy daughter, which thou hast supposed
Would be my wife. This youth is your lost son –
Who is mine heir, as I alway disposed –
Thou carried in thy body many a month.
I kept them in Bologna, known to none.
Take them again, and here I swear to you,
You ne'er will lose again these children two.
And those who spake much evil against me,
I warn them well that I have done this deed
Not out of malice, nor for cruelty,
But for to try in thee thy womanhood,
And not to slay my children – God forbid! –
But I have kept them privily and still
While I assayed thy constancy and will.

GRISILDE.
O tender loves! O dear young children mine,
I had believed so sure and steadfastly
That cruel hounds, or scavenging vermin
Had eaten you. But God of his mercy,
And your devoted father, tenderly
Hath kept you safe –

CLERK.
And in a sudden swound
She faints away and sinks down to the ground.

Music. WALTER *and the* CHILDREN *recover her. She is dressed richly and set at the table on* WALTER*'s right-hand side, her* DAUGHTER *next to her, her* SON *next to his* FATHER, *reflecting the heavily Christian iconography of the story.*

Full many a year in high prosperity
Lived man and wife in concord, ever blest.
And richly his daughter married he
Unto a lord – one of the worthiest
In all Italia. Then in peace and rest
Old Janicle within his court he kept
Til that the soul out of his body crept.
His son succeeded in his heritage
And reigned in peace after his father's day
And fortunate was in his marriage
But put not his own wife in such assay.
The world is not so strong – ye can't say nay –
As it hath been in olden times of yore,
And constancy's less widespread than before.

CHAUCER.

Grisild is dead, and with her died patience
And both are buried now in Italy
For which I say to you, our audience,
Let no man follow Walter's policy,
In hopes his wife hath Grisild's constancy,
For he must fail, and fail most piteously.

So when this worthy clerk his tale had told
Our Host cried out and swore:

HOST.

Now by God's nails!
Rather than have a pocketful of gold,
I wish my wife had listened to that tale!

MERCHANT.

So do I mine – for so it fares with me.
I have a wife, the worst that there could be.

HOST.

Then, Merchant, since you know so much their art,
Full heartily, I pray you, tell us part.

MERCHANT.

Gladly I will, but not of mine own woe,
That would I most forget – as God doth know!

Sixteen: The Merchant's Tale

MERCHANT.
Whilom there dwelt a man in Lombardy,
A worthy knight that born was in Pavee
And there he lived in great prosperity –
Full sixty years a wifeless man was he,
Following always his bodily delight
On women, as and when his appetite
Tickled this wayward lord to scratch his itch.
After his sixtieth year – I know not which
It was: fear of Judgement Day or dotage –
There grew within his heart so strong an urge,
An all consuming need, for to be wed –
To take one woman, lawfully, to bed.

JANUARY.
Now certainly, as sure as God is King,
To take a wife, it is a glorious thing –
A wife that's young – a wife both young and fair –
On which I might engender me an heir.
Our God on high – when he had Adam makëd,
And saw him all alone and belly-naked,
God of his love and goodness spake thus then:
'Let us now make an help meet for this man
Like to himself.' And so he made him Eve.
Here may ye see, and hereby may you prove
A wife is a man's comfort, his support,
His Earthly Paradise, and lustiest sport –
A wife! Saint Mary, benedicite!
How might a man e're know adversity
That hath a wife? He can know none, say I!
My friends, I fear I'm almost at Pit's brink,
Now give me your advice. Say what ye think.
She shall not be past twenty years – a dish
Of young sweet flesh! I'll taste no stinking fish.
I'll have no woman thirty year of age –
That's dry bean-straw unfit for horse forage –
And no old widows – I'll have none of such
They are too cunning – they know far too much.

PLACEBO.

Ah brother January, brother dear,
You have no need of counsel from us here.
You are so wise – so full of sapience
The world hath always known you for prudence.
Do now in this matter just as ye list
Whatever you decide will be the best.

JANUARY.

I have my eye, upon a girl called May –

JUSTINIUS.

Now brother mine, be patient, I ye pray,
And listen carefully to what I say.
Seneca, one reputed worldly wise,
Saith that a man should listen to advice
Before disposing of his goods and wealth.
And if ye wed – and this ye know yourself –
You give your goods – and more: yourself – away.
I warn you brother it is no child's play.

JANUARY.

My mind's made up. I'm going to marry May.

JUSTINIUS.

Whom you know nothing of. Men must enquire
If she be wise, and chaste, a drunk, a liar,
Or proud – how if she turns out shrewish? –
Sullen and cloudy, angry or mannish –
How do you know she won't waste all thy goods?
Let me enquire of her. I think you should,
Take time to pause. Consider many a day –

JANUARY.

Well thank ye, brother. Have you had your say?
A straw for Seneca! – the man's an ass!
His words aren't worth a nosebag-full of grass!
Would you school me? Far wiser men than thou,
As thou hast heard, assented here just now
To what I want. Placebo, what say ye?

PLACEBO.

I say that man is cursed – upon my life –
That comes between a husband and his wife.

JUSTINIAN.
Do your will. You think this girl's a treasure?
The man who weds in haste, repents at leisure.
The only saving grace that I can see
Is that she may become your purgatory!
And thus God means that she shall be His whip,
So that your soul shall straight to heaven skip.

MERCHANT.
The bonds are quickly sealed. The wedding day
Is come, and Janu'ry in rich array
With his young wife is to the church door went
Where they receive the holy sacrament.
Out comes the priest with stole about his neck.

PRIEST (*to* MAY).
I bid you be like Sarah or Rebekk.
In wisdom – faithful to this man, your lord.
And now kneel down and hear the word of God.

They are married – a wedding feast.

SONG.
All night neath the rose bush, the rose bush
All night neath the rose bush I lay
Durst I not pluck a rose from the rose bush
But I bore yet her flower away

JANUARY.
For God's love, boy, as soon as it may be,
Make my guests void the house, in courteous wise.

DAMYAN.
I shall do so, Lord – somewhat I'll devise.

JANUARY.
I am in haste – why else did I marry? –
I would to bed, and will no longer tarry.

MERCHANT.
In joy and bliss went homeward every man
Except this boy – this squire, Damyan
Who'd carved before this old knight many a day.
He was so ravished on his lady, May,

That for the very pain he was nigh wood,
He almost died, or fainted where he stood,
So sore had Venus burned him with her brand.

MAY *goes to bed, accompanied by her* MAIDS.

JANUARY.
Now help me Damyan. Give me your hand.

DAMYAN *helps lift* JANUARY *from the table, then helps him into his nightgown.*

MERCHANT.
And to his bed went Damyan hastily,
Namore of him at this time need I say –
We'll leave him there to weep and to complain
Hoping that May will pity all his pain.

JANUARY *gets into bed with* MAY.

And January fast in his arms doth take
His fresh young May, a paradise to make.
He lulleth her, he kisseth her full oft.
With tough thick bristles in his beard unsoft –
Like to the skin of houndfish, sharp as thorns
He scrapes her tender face, slobbers and fawns,
And whispers in her ear:

JANUARY.
Alas! Alas!
I must to you, my dear, do great trespass.
I fear I shall offend, and cause you pain
Before this thing of mine sinks down again.
But nonetheless – pray take it patiently,
For there's no workman, whosoere he be,
That does his job both well and hastily –
I'll take my time and do all perfectly.
Who cares how long it takes – how long we play?
A man may do no sin with his own wife,
Nor hurt himself while using his own knife.

MERCHANT.
But God knows what May thought, deep in her heart,
When she beheld him slipping off his shirt,

Scratching his scrawny neck, nightcap on head.
She rated not a bean his sports in bed.

Meanwhile this Damyan in Venus' fire
So burns he almost dyeth from desire,
And so decides his life he'll aventüre –
No longer might he such torments endure.
Full secretly a pen he goes and borrows
And in a letter sets down all his sorrows,
In poetry writ – a long complaining lay –
Unto his fair, his fresh young lady, May.
Then, in a purse of silk, inside his shirt
He doth it hide, pressed close against his heart.

JANUARY *dresses, helped by a* PAGE.

JANUARY.
Too tight! Saint Marie! Say, how may it be
That Damyan, my squire attends not me?
Is he sick, boy? Or how may it betide?

PAGE.
Yes, sick, My Lord – a sudden grave sickness –
That's why I'm here to do his bisynesse.
No other cause would keep him from your side.

JANUARY.
Yea, so I think. In bed then let him bide.
He is a gentil squire, by my truth!
If he should die it were great shame and routhe.
To visit him in sick-bed were good deed.
Madame, my wife! Come hither, May, take heed:
Go call your women – visit Damyan,
And sport with him. He is a gentil man.
And comfort him in sickness where he lies.

MERCHANT.
Up to his chamber then the lady hies,
With all her women, up to Damyan,
Down by his bedside goes and sits she then.

DAMYAN *holds her hand and, unseen by the* WOMEN, *slips it under his shirt. Guided by him, she takes the silk purse and removes the letter.*

DAMYAN.

Have mercy, Lady – don't discover me
For I am dead if he that letter see.

Leaving the LADIES *with* DAMYAN, *she goes into the privy and reads the letter.*

MAY.

O Damyan!
Here do I swear – whoever I displease,
I'll find the means his piteous heart to ease.
I care for no man else – him I assure
To love him best of any creäture.
Though he were poor – had nothing but his shirt –
I'd pity him and give him all my heart.

She tears the letter and drops it down the jakes.

MERCHANT.

This gentle May, o'erflown with piteousness
Wrote him a letter full of tenderness
In which she promised him her every grace.
Now they lacked nothing – only time and place
Where she might unto all his lust submit –
He might swyve her – if he could manage it.

She returns and conceals her letter about his person, unseen by her LADIES.

PAGE.

My Lady. My Lord calls for you.

MAY.

Farewell!
Damyan, I hope, that you will soon be whole.

Exit with LADIES. DAMYAN *leaps out of bed, sings, dresses, combs his hair.* MAY *returns to* JANUARY *who drags her off to the garden for sex.*

MERCHANT.

This noble Janu'ry lived the life of kings.
Among such others of his noble things
He had a garden, walled around with stone –
A fairer garden was there never none

Furnished with fountains, hedged with laurels green.
Full many a time King Pluto and his Queen
Prosérpina, and all their fayerye
Would sport themselves, and maken melody
About those fountains, and dance – so men told.
This noble knight, this Janu'ry the old
Took such delight to walk therein and play,
That he allowed no wight to bear the key
Save he himself. The gate locked fast he kept,
And when he burned to pay his wife her debt
In summer's season, thither would he go
With May his wife – no other but they two –
And certain things he had not tried in bed
He would, at length, perform them there instead.

O mishap sudden! Fortune changeable,
Like to the scorpion, black deceivable,
That flatt'rest with thine head when thou wilt sting,
Thy tail is death, through its envenoming.
Alas! This noble January free
In midst of lust, and his prosperity,
Is struck stone blind – and that right suddenly.

JANUARY.
Alack! I'm blind! And nothing can I see!

MERCHANT.
He weepeth and he waileth piteously,
And fell into a mighty jealousy,
Lest that young May should into mischief slide.
And so he kept her ever by his side
And would not suffer her to ride or go
But that his hand was on her evermoe.
For which full often wept this fair young May
For she loved Damyan outrageously.
Unless that she could have him as she list
She knew she'd die – her very heart would burst.
Upon the other side poor Damyan
Became the sorrowfullest wretched man
That ever was. For neither night nor day
Could ever Damyan speak a word to May.

But nonetheless, by writing to and fro
And privy signs they plotted what to do.

MAY *removes the key to the garden from* JANUARY, *gives it to* DAMYAN *and indicates that, using candle-wax he should make a copy of it. Which he does.*

The key he counterfeits, and hastily,
Will let him in the garden secretly.
Eight days before the month of June was gone,
When days were warm and brightly shone the sun,
Upon a morrow, said this Janu'ry:

JANUARY.
Rise up my wife, my love, my lady free,
The turtle's voice is heard, my dove, my sweet,
Winter is gone with his rains cold and wet.
Come forth now – be mine eyes, my Columbine!
O how much fairer are thy breasts than wine!
My garden is enclosèd all about,
Come forth my milk-white spouse, for out of doubt
Thou hast me wounded to my heart, O wife!
Be true to me, I'll love you all my life.

MERCHANT.
Such lewd old words he'd got out of a book.
Young May gave Damyan many a sign and look,
That he should go before them with his key,
And clamber up into the old pear tree.
As soon as he sees what she means, he's gone.
This January, blind as any stone,
With May upon his arm and no wyght moe
Into the garden makes all haste to go
And locks the gate behind him suddenly.

JANUARY.
Now, May, there's no one here but thou and I.
Be true to me – and shall I tell thee why?
Thou shalt gain, certain, great richesse thereby.
I swear to you, my love, on my honour,
That all my heritage, both town and tower,
I'll give to you – make charters as ye list.
It shall be done tomorrow ere sun rest,

To prove my love – thou know'st it out of doubt.
Now kiss me, wife, and let us roam about.

MAY.
Why speak ye thus? How could I be untrue?
I have a soul to lose as well as you.
Did I not, husband, put me in thine hand
When that the priest to you my body bound?
If I grow false – if I my honour lack –
Then strap me up and tie me in a sack,
And in the nearest river let me drench.
I am a loyal wife, no slut nor wench.

JANUARY.
I love you best, and never shall no other.

MAY.
Beneath this pear-tree let's lie down together.

MERCHANT.
Bright was the day, and blue the firmament
Phoebus his golden beams had downward sent
To gladden every flower with his warmness –
He was that time in Gemini, I guess.
It happed, as I have told you, everyone,
That some days in that garden – this was one –
The Fairy King would come to sport and play
With many a lady in his company
Following his wife, his queen, Prosérpina –
She that he ravished once from Etna,
While that she gathered flowers in the mede.
In Claudian you may the story read.

PLUTO.
My wife, look there. Ye may not say me nay,
Experience will show, nigh every day,
What treasons women will commit on men.
Ten thousand thousand could I tell of them.
Do you not see that honourable knight?
Because he's old, and hath quite lost his sight
He will be cuckolded by his own squire.

MAY.
Alas! Alas, that I can reach no higher!

I fain would eat one of those pears I see –
Or I shall die! I long so dreadfully
To suck the little pears – they're firm and round –
Alas, I may not reach them from the ground.

JANUARY.
What can we do? There is no boy, you see,
Who could climb up. Alas that it should be
That I am blind!

MAY.
Well, sir, it matters not.
And yet, my ancient love – I'll tell thee what! –
If you'd vouchsafe me now, for God's sweet sake,
The pear tree firmly in your arms to take,
Then could I climb up well enough, I swear.
Give me your hands – hold me the tree-trunk – there –
Then will I set my foot upon your back.

JANUARY.
Certés, my love. Thereon should be no lack
If I could help you with my true heart's blood.

She climbs into the tree. DAMYAN *lifts up her smock and swyves her.*

PLUTO.
Look what that harlot's doing in the tree!
Now will I grant here, of my majesty,
Unto this old, this blind and worthy knight
That he, once more, shall have his two eyes' sight.
Since that his wife hath done him villainy,
Then shall he know her and her harlotry,
Both in reproof of her and others too.

Pears rain down from the tree.

PROSERPINA.
Ye shall, My Lord? Would you do so?
I am a woman, therefore I must speak,
Or else I'll swell until my heart shall break.
Now, by the soul of Jupiter, I swear
I will not leave her trapped and speechless there,
But give her sharp words and a ready wit.

Whate're he may accuse she'll answer it.
And every woman after for her sake –
Even the ones that in their guilt are take –
With brazen face they shall themselves excuse
And bear them down that would their wives accuse.

JANUARY.
A miracle! A miracle! I can see!
Where are you May?

MAY.
Someone's coming!

DAMYAN.
It's me!

JANUARY *and* DAMYAN.
Aghhhhhhh!

JANUARY.
Out! Help! Alas! Harrow! What do I see!
O brazen Lady Lechery what d'ye do!

MAY.
What do you mean, sir? What? What aileth you?
Have patience, sir – be easy in your mind
For by my means you are no longer blind.
On peril of my soul, I tell no lies,
A wizard told me how to heal your eyes.
The only way, he said, to make you see
Was to struggle with a man up in a tree.
God knows I've done all with the best intent!

JANUARY.
Struggle? Struggle! I saw it! In it went!
Shame on you both! And as for him – he dies!
He was swyving you – I saw it with mine eyes!
Swyving I say – or I'll be hanged, and nailed!

MAY.
Well then, I waste my time – my med'cine's failed.
For I am sure, if you could really see
You would not dare address such words to me.
You only glimpsed – you've not your perfect sight.

JANUARY.

O I can see – as well as ever I might,
Thanks be to God! – with these mine eyes – these two –
And, by my truth, I thought he swyved thee so.

MAY.

You're mazed, you're mazed, good sir. Ah me!
This is the thanks I get to make you see!
Alas that ever tried I to be kind!

She sobs, DAMYAN *comforts her.*

JANUARY.

There, there, my dear, now put it from your mind.
Come down, my love, and if I have spoke ill,
God help me so, it was not by my will.
But, by my father's soul, I could have sworn
Young Damyan was giving me the horn,
And lifted up thy smock above his breast.

MAY.

Think what you will. I thought all for the best.
But, sir, a man that waketh from long sleep
At first sees nothing clearly – out he peeps –
His sight is blurred, confused, all shapes are one,
But he regains his vision ere too long –
Right so a man that long time blind hath been.
For when his sight hath newly come again
His vision's cloudy for some little while –
Many imagined sights might him beguile.
Take heed, I pray you, for by Heaven's King
There's many a man believes he's seen a thing,
When things are often not the things they seem.
You shouldn't judge until you're sure, I ween.

MERCHANT.

And with those words they came down from the tree.
This January who is glad but he?
He kissed his wife, the three of them went home.
And thus my tale of January is done
God bless us all, and bless us all His Mother,
Here ends my tale. Let someone tell another.

HOST.
Hey, what a slut! Now God some mercy show,
And all such wives let's pray He'll keep us fro!
Lo, now you see what sleights and subtleties
Lurk in a woman! They're like busy bees
Buzzing away, us poor men to deceive,
And from the truth they ever warp and weave.
Young squire, come near, if that your will it be
And say something of love. I'm sure that ye
Know much of love – nay, more than any man.

SQUIRE.
Not so, sir. Yet I'll do the best I can
With all my heart. For I would not rebel
Against your choice. Therefore my tale I'll tell.
And pray excuse me if I fail in this
My intentions are good, though I may miss
Bits out – I'm not sure I can remember it. Er . . .
In Russia . . . no that's not it.
Er . . .

PRIORESS (*feeding her* DOG).
Pretty, pretty, pretty little puppy wuppykins . . .

Seventeen: The Squire's Tale

SQUIRE.
At Sarray, in the land of Tartary – that's it –
At Sarray in the land of Tartary
There dwelt a king that made war on Russee,
In which there died full many a doughty man,
This noble king was called . . . er . . .

CHAUCER.
Kubla Khan?

SQUIRE.
Cambyuskan.

CHAUCER.
Ah.

SQUIRE.
This Cambyuskan of which I have you told
Against the sword of winter, keen and cold.

Pause.

In royal vestments sat upon a dais
With diadem, full high in his palace . . .
I'm sorry I've forgotten it – just the next bit
A knight comes into the hall . . . in his palace
And gives him three presents:
A horse made of brass that can fly,
A mirror in which he can see the truth in men's souls,
And a ring, which he gives to his daughter . . . er . . .

CHAUCER.
Canacee?

SQUIRE.
Yes, Canacee – and with the ring she can understand
The language of birds. That's the best bit.
She sees a falcon on a tree, wounding herself because she's in love –

PRIORESS.
Canacee or the falcon?

SQUIRE.
What?

PARDONER.
Is it Canacee or the falcon that's in love?

SQUIRE.
The falcon. She's been deserted by her tercelet.

SUMMONER.
Her what?

SQUIRE.
Tercelet – you know, a kind of hawk.
It really is quite good, if I can remember it – Ah wait –
First will I tell you of Cambyuscan

That in his time, had many a city won,
And after I will speak of Algarsif,
And how he won Theodora to his wife
For whom full oft in great peril he was,
Had he not been helped out by the steed of brass
And after will I speak of Cambalo –

PRIORESS.
Must you? –

SQUIRE.
That fought in lists with both the brethren two
For Canacee, so that he might her win,
And where I left I will again begin:
Apollo whirled his golden car so high
Til in god's house – Mercurius the sly . . . er . . .
At Sarray in the land of Tartary
There dwelt a king that made war on Russee
In which there died full many a doughty man,
This noble king was called . . . er . . .

FRANKLIN.
In faith, young man, thou hast thee well acquit
And gentlemanly – I praise well thy wit.
So feelingly you speak, and that's the truth –
We must make some allowance for your youth –
And yet you spoke your speeches daintily.
I have a son, and by the Trinity,
Would he were possessed of such discretion
As you are, sir.

HOST.
Well, Franklin, since this interruption
Seems to suggest that you have much to say,
I pray you tell your tale without delay –
You know you'll have to sometime – that's our rule.

FRANKLIN.
Gladly, sir Host. I shall obey your will.
I hope to God that it will please you all
And if I fail I have not far to fall.

Eighteen: The Franklin's Tale

FRANKLIN.
In Armorik, that we should call Brittane,
There was a knight who loved, and took great pain
To serve a lady with great diligence
And many a labour, without recompense,
He for his lady wrought ere she was won.
She was one of the fairest under sun,
And came of such a proud and noble line
'Twas with great trepidation he, in time,
Began to tell his woes, pain, and distress.
And she, at last, seeing his worthiness,
Decided such a love should have reward.
She took him for her husband and her lord,
Or such lordship men have over their wives.
Yet for to lead the more in bliss their lives. He said:

ARVERAGUS.
Of my free will I swear, as I am knight,
That never in my life, by day nor night,
Will I take on myself the mastery
'Gainst your will, nor fall prey to jealousy.
I will obey you, follow where you lead,
As any lover to his lady should –
Save that the name and show of sovereignty,
That must I keep, for shame of my degree.
In all things else I'll serve with humbleness.

DORIGEN.
My love, my lord since of your gentillesse
You offer me so free and large a rein
Never, betwixt us two, may God ordain
Come, through my fault, discord at home, nor strife.
I am always your faithful, humble wife.
Have here my truth, while heart beats in my breast.

FRANKLIN.
And so they lived in quiet and in rest.
There is one thing, sirs, we may safely say:
That friends should each the other one obey

If they would love, and long keep company.
Love will not be constrained by mastery –
When mast'ry comes, the god of love anon
Beateth his wings, and 'Farewell!' he is gone!
Love is a thing as any spirit free.
Women – all women – desire liberty
And so do men. That's the difficulty.
In perfect love and great prosperity
Home with his wife he went to his country,
Not far from Pedmark, there his dwelling was
Where long they lived in bliss and great solas
That sometimes comes 'twixt husbands and their wives.
Nigh on two year they lead their blissful lives,
Till Arveragus – that's the young knight's name –
Must go to England – we should say Briteyne –
To seek in arms great worship and renown,
'Twould be two years ere he saw wife and home.
What shall I say of Dorigen his wife
Who loved her young lord as she loved her life?
She mourns, and weeps, and wails, and feels such pain
That will not ease till he come home again.

FIRST LADY.
I pray you, Madame, leave this heaviness.
I fear that you will slay yourself, alas!

SECOND LADY.
Pray come and walk with us in company –
Let's drive away your darker fantasies.

FIRST LADY.
Hath not your lord, to banish all your care
Sent letters home that tell of his welfare?
And that he will, ere long, be home again?

DORIGEN.
And had he not, my sorrow had me slain.

SECOND LADY.
Come walk with us. Come! Grant us our request.

DORIGEN.
Well then I will. It may be for the best.

FRANKLIN.

The castle where they lived o'erlooked the sea
And, with her ladies, on the cliffs walked she
Where many a barge and many a sailing ship
Breasting the foaming waves both tall and deep,
She saw – and stood to watch them come and go.
But sight of them increaseth all her woe.

DORIGEN.

Of all those many ships there is not one
That hath on board my love to bring him home.

FRANKLIN.

Thoughts came upon her that she would not think,
Then would she cast her eyes down from the brink,
But when she saw the rocks, grisly and black
In sudden fear her heart began to quake.

DORIGEN.

Eternal God, that through Thy providence
Leadest the world by wisest governance,
Ye nothing make, men say, from idleness.
But, Lord, those fiendish rocks – what's their purpose?
They seem some devil's black confusiön
And no works of Your fair Creatiön.
No good dwells in them, north, south, west nor east –
They're home to no man, neither bird nor beast.
They foster nought, yet everything annoy.
See Ye not, Lord, how they mankind destroy?
An hundred thousand souls, drowned in the sea,
Have those rocks slain, known only unto Thee –
Men made in Thine image – Your fairest work
Ground in those stony teeth – lost in the murk.
Mankind is told of Your great charity
Towards them. But I ask how can it be
That Ye such means make for destruction –
That bring such good to such corruption?
Churchmen and scholars may say what they list,
And prove from Holy Writ all's for the best –
How it may be is not for me to know.
But Thou, Great God, that makes the winds to blow,
Keep safe my lord! That's all my conclusion.

Churchmen and scholars, pardon my confusion.
O would to God that these sharp rocks and black
Were sunk i'th'pit of hell for my love's sake!

FRANKLIN.
Her ladies learned 'twas no good policy
To let their mistress wander by the sea,
And so they fell to think of different sports –
Dancing, and games at chess, and other sorts.

Upon a time, early in morning-tide,
Unto a garden at the castle's side
They went to dance and feast all the long day –
It was, I think, the sixth morning of May,
Which May had painted with his soft warm showers
This garden full of leaves and fragrant flowers –
It overflowed with beauty and pleasance.
And when they'd dined they all got up to dance,

A dance.

And play and sing. Save Dorigen alone,
Who sat and sighed and wished she could be gone,
For in the dance was one man played no part:
I mean her husband, he who ruled her heart.

And in this dance, amongst the other men,
There danced a squire in view of Dorigen,
That fresher was, and jollier of array
Than, in my judgement, is the month of May,
Young, strong, right virtuous, fair, and rich, and wise.
And loved by all, and holden in great prize.
And, if I must tell true, and tell I shall –
Though Dorigen knew nought of this at all –
This lusty squire, this servant of Venus,
Which that yclepéd was Aurelius,
Had burned in love with her for two long years.
He never showed his love and hid his tears,
And of his pain he never durst her tell,
He drank his cup of grief – the cup as well –
In his despair. For nothing would he say,
Save in his songs he would his heart betray –
A little of it – just general bewailing:

He said he loved, and that his love was failing –
That sort of thing – I'm sure you know the stuff
For in our youth we hear it often enough.
But nonetheless it happ'd as they went hence
They fell in conversation by chance,
And, with a pounding heart, Aurelius
Who saw his time had come, addressed her thus:

AURELIUS.
Madame, by God that knoweth me and sees
I would do anything that might you please,
I wish, that day that your Arveragus,
Went o'er the seas, that I, Aurelius
Had reached the land from whence there's no return.
Too well I knew this love of mine you'd spurn –
Offering me nothing but a broken heart.
O Madame, pity me my sharp pain's smart,
For with one word you may me slay or save.
Here at your feet, would God I'd made my grave!
I've no words more, nor time to speak them in.
Have mercy, sweet, and think my love no sin.

DORIGEN.
May I believe you speak in your right mind?
I ne'er suspected I should ever find,
In you, Aurelius, such an ill intent.
Do I mistake? – The words you spoke you meant?
Now by our God that gave me soul and life
The last thing I would be's an untrue wife
In word, nor deed, as long as I have wit.
Forever I am his to whom I'm knit.
This answer you shall ever have of me.
Yet, poor Aurelius, by God above,

Teases gently, as if he's a spoilt child.

I would perhaps agree to be your love,
Since now I see how piteous you complain.
Upon that day that from around Britayne
You take away the black rocks, stone by stone,
So that they sink no ship, nor boat goes down –
I say, when you have made the coastline clean

Of rocks – no single stone must there be seen –
Then will I love you best of any man.
Have here mine oath – it's all the truth I can.

AURELIUS.
Is there no other grace in you, Lady?

DORIGEN.
None. None – I swear it by Him that made me.

AURELIUS.
Madame, your sentence is my death, I see,
Tempting me with impossibility.

She exits, pitying him. AURELIUS*, in despair, goes into the temple of Apollo and throws himself at the foot of Apollo's statue.*

AURELIUS.
Apollo! God, and wisest governor
Of every herb and plant, and tree and flower,
Look down upon thy servant lost and lorn! –
Lo, Lord, my death is by my Lady sworn
Unless, bright god, of thy benignity,
Unto my dying heart you show pity.
For well I wot, Apollo, if you list
It is your help that would avail me best.
O do some miracle, lest my heart brake –
I'll walk barefoot to Delphi for your sake!
Look, as I speak how tears pour down my cheeks.
O, on my pain have some compassion!

FRANKLIN.
And with that word he falls down in a swoon.
His brother came, and to his bed him brought.
So in despair, in torment and sad thought,
There must we let this woeful creature lie.
I cannot tell if he will live or die.

Arveragus, in health, with great honour,
Now judged by all of chivalry the flower
Is comen home! O worthiest of men!
How blissful artow now, O Dorigen,
That hast thy lusty husband in thine arms!

This fresh young knight, hath come unscathed through harms,
And loves thee as he loves his own heart's life.

ARVERAGUS.
O Dorigen, my joy, my love, my wife!

FRANKLIN.
And thus in joy and bliss we'll let them dwell
And of the sick Aurelius will I tell.
In languor and in torments furious
Two year and more lay poor Aurelius
And none could guessed the cause of his dolour
Save his brother, a gentleman and scholar.
It came into this brother's remembrance
That, while he was at Orleans in France,
He'd seen a book of which he fell in awe
Belonging to a fellow man of law.
It was a book of natural magic's craft
Which in his study had his fellow left,
Which book spake much of operations
Touching the eight and twenty mansions
Belonging to the moon – such secret lore
As Holy Church enjoins us to deplore.
And when this book came to his remembrance
Anon for joy his heart began to dance.

BROTHER.
My brother shall recover, certainly,
And I'll accomplish it right secretly,
For I am sure that there be sciences
To cunningly deceive appearances –
Tricks an illusionist knows how to play.
For oft, at feasts – or so I've heard men say –
These subtle tricksters have flooded the hall
And set a barge upon it – oars and all –
And men have rowed upon it up and down.
Sometimes they conjure up a grim lion,
Sometimes spring flowers as if it were a mede,
Sometimes a vine with grapes both white and red,
Sometimes a castle, all of lime and stone –
Yet, as men look, these visions all are gone,
Or so these things appear to human sight.

Thus I conclude, it may be that I might
At Orleans, my fellow student find
That keeps these moony mansions in his mind.
His magic skills, I pray to gods above,
Will win Aurelius his lady's love.
For with illusions to deceive the eye
A cunning man might clear all Brittany
Of every rock that's set along its coast.
And if the vision hold – two weeks at most –
Then were my brother eased of all his woe:
His love must do his will – she can't say no.

FRANKLIN.
Well there it is – what needeth wordës moe?
To Orleans in haste the two repair,
In hopes to rid Aurelius of his care.
As they drew near the town a youth they met:

SCHOLAR.
I know why you have come. Say nothing yet.
I've read, Aurelius, of your desires
Your story's written in the starry fires.
But come home to my house and take your ease
Your chambers are prepared. Come – if you please.

They go to the house and a meal is served. The YOUNG MAGICIAN *conjures up several visions for their entertainment. First a park with hounds bringing down a stag. Then falconry, then jousting knights.*

FRANKLIN.
Before their eyes illusions gan appear
Forest and parks where roamed the antlered deer –
A hundred of them slain by coupled hounds
And some with arrows bled with bitter wounds
And some with hawks pursued the heronshaw,
Then armed knights jousting in lists they saw.

SCHOLAR.
Now all these sights were brought for your pleasance.
What else would ye see?

AURELIUS.
My lady in a dance.

Music. A dance. Then DORIGEN *joins the dance.* AURELIUS *gets up and dances with her very lovingly. At last the* SCHOLAR *claps his hands and the vision disappears.*

Master, now say, what sum shall I pay thee
For clearing all the rocks from Britaynee
From Gironde to the Seine's wide estuary?

SCHOLAR.
A thousand pounds. To less I can't agree –
And even then I'd do it reluctantly.

AURELIUS.
A thousand pound! Fie on a thousand pound!
The whole wide world – which now men say is round –
I would you give if I were lord of it –
The bargain is well driv'n – for we be knit.
Ye shall be paid in full, so shall I swear.
And this I pray – let us not linger here,
I would be gone in haste tomorrow morn.

SCHOLAR.
And thou shalt have thy lady, I'll be sworn.

CHRISTMAS SONG.
Conditor alme siderum
Eterna lux credencium
Christe, redemptor omnium
Exaudi preces supplicum.

Vergente mundi vespere
Uti sponsus de thalamo
Egressus honestissima
Virginis matris clausula.

Te deprecamur, agie
Venture judex seculi,
Conserva nos in tempore
Hostis a telo perfidy.

FRANKLIN.
Phoebus wax old, and hued is like laton
That in his hotter declination

Once shone like burnished gold in streams of light
But now his shining's pale, I dare well sayn
The bitter frosts, the icy sleets and rain,
Destroyeth all the green in tree and sward.
Janus sits by the fire with snow-white beard
And sippeth from his bugle-horn red wine –
The boar's head's set on board where he would dine,
And 'Sing Nowel!' cries every lusty man.

This subtle scholar, with all the skill he can,
Plotted the stars and drew conclusions,
Found favourable times for his illusions,
So that by art – or was it jugglery? –
Who knows what truth lies in astrology? –
That she and every wight would see and say
The rocks of Brittany were washed away,
Or else sunk under sea, deep in the ground.
And very soon propitious times he found
To work his tricks. And in a week or twey
It seemed as if the rocks melted away.

AURELIUS (*throwing himself at the* SCHOLAR*'s feet*).
How can this woeful wretch, Aurelius
Thank you enough? – And mighty Lord Apollo
That warmed my heart when it grew cold and hollow.

FRANKLIN.
And to Apollo's house his way makes he
Knowing that there he should his lady see.
With pounding, fluttering heart and humble cheer
Aurelius salutes his lady dear:

AURELIUS.
Mine own lady, behold this wretched man –
Know that I dread and love as best I can,
And in this world the loathest would I be
To displease you. But as you know and see
I stand here sick with love – wasted and wan,
At point of death – I am so woebegone –
And I will die indeed unless you hear me.
You'd slay me with a look – yet do not fear me:
If you command I'll keep me from your sight,

Nor will I challenge aught of you by right,
All that I'll take, I take it of your grace,
For in a garden once – you know the place –
Ye wot right well what then ye bid me do
And in mine hand ye placed your own hand – so –
And swore – God knows you did – to love me best
Although I know mine own unworthiness.
Madame, your honour holds my life in pawn.
My life's of no account – Yet, you have sworn . . .
I have done all as you commanded me.
And, if it pleases you, you may go see.
Do as you list, but keep your oath in mind:
Slay me, or save me – no rocks will ye find.
Repent your cruelty – there's God above –
Take time to pause before you kill your love.

Exit.

DORIGEN.
Alas! Alas, that ever this should hap!
I little thought to fall in such a trap.
Who would believe it possibility
That such a marvel, or catastrophe,
Against all nature still, might come to pass!

FRANKLIN.
She gets her home, crying ever 'Alas!'
And piteous weeps and wails the whole day through
For very fear – there's nothing she can do.
She grows so pale it's pity for to see
For gone from home was good Arveragus,
So to herself she spake and reasoned thus:

DORIGEN.
O cruel Fortune, on thee I complain!
Why am I thus entangled in thy chain?
From which to free myself I know no way
Save only dishonour – Or else I slay
Myself. One of these two I must now choose.
Yet there's no choice! My life I'd rather lose
Than give my body over to such shame,
And know that I am false, or lose my name,

When with my death I may be quit, ywis.
Hath there not many a woeful wife ere this,
And many a maiden, slain herself – Alas! –
Rather than with her body do trespass?

FRANKLIN.
Thus plaineth Dorigen for many a day,
Her purpose was that she herself would slay.
When Arveragus is at last come home
And asks her why she weeps and maketh moan.

DORIGEN.
Alas the day that ever I was born!
Thus have I done, my love – thus have I sworn –

FRANKLIN.
She tells him all that ye have heard before –
It needeth not rehearsing anymore.

ARVERAGUS.
Poor Dorigen. Is there aught else but this?

DORIGEN.
Aught else, my lord? It is enough, ywis,
Nay and too much, and 'twere God's will!

ARVERAGUS.
Ye say the truth. Then let what sleeps sleep still.
All may be well perchance, yet, come what may,
You cannot break your oath. Now, by my fey,
As may our God have mercy on us both –
I'd rather stab myself than not speak truth –
The love I bear you bids me send you forth.
Without our truth we two are nothing worth.
Truth is the highest thing a man must keep –

DORIGEN.
My lord, my love! Alas, you weep, you weep –

ARVERAGUS.
But I forbid you here, on pain of death,
That never, while life lasts and we draw breath,
To no wight tell thou of this aventúre.
As best I may I will my grief endure.

And in my face betray no heaviness
That folk think harm of us, or worse may guess.
I'll fetch my squire. Then go and call your maid,
They'll go with you. There's no more to be said.

The SQUIRE *and the* MAID *are called.* ARVERAGUS *and* DORIGEN *embrace, then* DORIGEN *goes towards the garden accompanied by the* MAID *and the* SQUIRE. AURELIUS *meets her in the street carrying rich presents for her.*

AURELIUS.
Where are you going, lady? Why so sad?

DORIGEN.
Unto the garden as my husband bade.
To keep my word to you – alas! Alas!

AURELIUS.
Madame, say to your lord Arveragus
That since I have seen his great gentillesse
To you – and seeing too your deep distress
That he had rather take shame on you both
Than ye to me should ever break your truth –
Say I had rather live my life in woe
Than rend apart the love betwixt you two.
I here release you, Madame, from your bond –
Quit all the powers you gave into my hand.
I plight my truth, I'll never you reprove
With what is past. And here I take my leave
Of you – the truest love and the best wife
That ever yet I knew in all my life.

She tries to speak but can't. She tries to kneel to him. He prevents her and exits.

FRANKLIN.
Arveragus and Dorigen his wife
In sovereign bliss forever led their life.
Never an angry word passed them between.
He cherished her as though she were a queen,
And she was true to him forevermore.
And of these two ye'll get from me no more.

Aurelius who hath in all ways lost,
Hath done a noble deed – but at what cost!

AURELIUS.
A thousand pounds in gold I've lost today
To this illusionist. What can I say?
For all mine heritage I needs must sell
And be a beggar. Here I may not dwell
To bring shame on my kindred in this place.
I've brought you gold – five hundred pounds I guess,
And I beseech you of your gentillesse,
Give me a year or two to find the rest.
I will pay all – at least I'll do my best.
If you will not, then I'm prepared to sell
My heritage. There is no more to tell.

SCHOLAR.
Say, did I not keep covenant with thee?
Did I not drown the rocks beneath the sea.

AURELIUS.
Ye did, ye did. I am the more to blame.

SCHOLAR.
And yet you had your lady all the same?

AURELIUS.
No. No. That I did not.

He sighs a four-beat sigh.

SCHOLAR.
What was the cause? Come. Tell me if you can.

FRANKLIN.
To tell his tale Aurelius began
And told him all as ye have seen before.
It needeth not to hear it any more –

AURELIUS.
I was at last o'ercome with such pity,
As freely as he sent his wife to me
I sent her back to him as free again.
And that is all. There is no more to sayn.

SCHOLAR.
Why then it seems to me my lever brother
Each of you was courteous as the other.
Sir, of the thousand pound I set you free.
I will not take a penny piece of thee.
You've lost enough. Farewell, and have good day.

FRANKLIN.
And so he took his horse and went his way.
Lordings, a question will I ask you now –
Which of those men behaved the best, say you?
Just think about it as our way we wend
I've said enough. My tale is at an end.

Applause – various reactions.

CHAUCER.
Lo, Canterbury's in sight! This little town
Is called by one and all Bob-up-and-down.

They ride on.

HOST.
Awake, thou sluggard Cook! God give you sorrow!
What aileth thou to sleep all through the morrow?
Hastow had fleas all night, or artow drunk?
Or hastow with some quean all night yswonke?

COOK.
How did he do't?

Very drunk – he can hardly stay on his horse.

CHAUCER.
How did who do what?

COOK (*lurches into the* HOST).
He!
How did he clear the rocks from Brittany?
Was he a fraud or was it alchemy?

He stumbles and grabs the SECOND NUN.

HOST.
O! Thy breath's foul stench will infect us all!

SECOND NUN.
Fie, stinking swine! Foul luck upon thee fall!
The minister and nurse unto all vice
The which men call in English 'idleness'
Is porter at the gate of avarice,
Lechery, wrath, envy, and drunkenness.
Only by prayer and moral cleanliness

COOK *lurches.*

May we escape the fiend who'd snare us all.
Only the vigilant escape a fall.

COOK *falls over.*

And for to turn us from such idleness
Which is a cause of much confusion,
I have here, with a faithful bisynesse,
Ta'en pains to make my own translation –
This is the life, the pains, the passion
Of she the garland bears – the rose, the lily –
'The Life and Martyrdom of Saint Cecily' –

COOK.
So where did they go to then – the rocks? Eh?

Lurches, knocks the manuscript out of her hand.

Was it a trick or was it alchemy?

CHAUCER.
It was a tale – a fable. That's all – nothing more.
Well here we are at Boggton under Blee.

They dismount at an inn. The SQUIRE *notices, with horror, that his horse has trampled to death the* PRIORESS*'s* LAPDOG.

Do I hear horses? Ah, who might this be?

Nineteen: The Canon's Yeoman's Interlude

The sound of galloping horses. Two men gallop up, sweating like pigs: The CANON *and his* YEOMAN.

CANON'S YEOMAN.
Whoa there, mine 'oss! Whoa there! Wee-hee!

CANON.
God save you all! Save all this companee!
Fast have I galloped, and all for your sake
Because I would your jolly band o'ertake,
And ride with you along to Canterb'ray.

HOST.
Then welcome, friend, and God gi'ye good-day.

CANON *goes into the inn, laughing. Obviously a jolly type.*

Your master seems as jocund as a jay.
He'll have a merry tale to tell, I'd say.

CHAUCER.
O not more tales! Is there to be no end to it?

HOST.
I pray thee tell me, is he a clerk or priest?

CANON'S YEOMAN.
Both priest and clerk but mostly Alchemist.
I've swunk and slaved for him nigh seven year:
Alchemy's secrets? We've come nowhere near!
All I once owned – I've lost the lot thereby,
And so, God knows, have many more than I.
Men ever seek great wealth, through easy means,
I tell you, get rich quick's the stuff of dreams.
Look at my face. It once was fresh and red.
Now I am wan, my colour's dull as lead.
That sliding science hath me made so bare
However hard I try, I get nowhere –
Nay, worse! I'm so indebted, for my pains,
Of gold I've borrowed, hoping still for gains,
That while I live I won't be free of debt.

Be warned by my example. Think on it.
A man who science tries will nothing win
Save pain, and empty purse, and wits worn thin.
And when he's spent his wealth and made no gain
He'll draw in other folk to do the same.
A man caught out by folly finds some ease
When fools around him share in his disease.

COOK.
So it wasn't alchemy, it was a trick?

Exit CANON'S YEOMAN.

CHAUCER.
It was whatever you want it to be!

HOST (*laughing at the* COOK).
O Bacchus, god of wine, I bless thy name
That can turn serious things into a game!
Worship and thanks be to thy deity!
And that's enough – press on to Canterbury!
Hey, Manciple! Tell us your tale I pray.

Twenty: The Manciple's Tale

A Miniature Opera.

MANCIPLE.
Well, sir, I will. Now listen to what I say.

Short overture.

When Lord Apollo dwelt on earth
The world was filled with light.
Apollo! Reason's first creator
Apollo! Everything that's bright.
Lord of the silver bow!

CHORUS.
Lord of the silver bow!

MANCIPLE.
He kept a crow. And the crow was white.

CROW (*singing sweetly*).
I'm white, I'm white. As you see I'm white.

CHORUS.
His crow was white.

MANCIPLE.
But music! Music! Music!
Was his delight.

CHORUS.
The lyre, the lute, all minstrelsy
Would Lord Apollo play. Such melody
Unheard today by any human ear,
He played upon his lyre:

APOLLO (*descends, playing a lyre*).
I am the Sun
Apollo
Light of reason
Delphi's potent lord
Curator of omniscience
The Far See-er
Born on Delos the wandering island
Wisdom's throne sea-anchored in truth's ocean.
Time's creator
I hold the orb of Time
Clockstopped
Its every bright facet fixed in perpetual play.
Time was; time is; and time
May be.

CROW.
Through dappled light of leafy grove
Pure sound ascends th' Olympian throne –

CHORUS.
Where Lord Apollo of the yellow hair,
Weeping, takes up his ivory inlaid lyre –

CHORUS *and* CROW.
There to accompany the immortal gods

Treading the mystic measures of heaven
Mingling our sorrow with their own.

APOLLO.
Sweet crow!

CROW.
Apollo!

Exit APOLLO.

CHORUS.
He'll feed you with ambrosia
When he returns.

CROW.
I'd rather feed on worms.

MANCIPLE.
Now lord Apollo had a wife
Which that he loved more than his life.
And night and day he pleased her

CROW.
He pleased her, as he squeezed her.

CHORUS.
Alas! Alas! Alas!
She was untrue –

CROW.
What! Who says so?

CHORUS.
She was untrue to him.
She had a lecherous appetite
On lower things took her delight
Though married to a god.

LOVER.
Lady will you lie with me?

WIFE.
Truly I will die with thee.

LOVER.
Lie with me.

WIFE.
Die with thee.

CROW.
Cuckoo! Cuckoo! Cuckoo!

CHORUS.
Flesh needs, other flesh that's new
Seeking some newfangledness

LOVER *and* LADY.
My (*Thy*) husband, may he never know
Keep him still in ignorance.

Exit.

CROW.
Cuckoo! Cuckoo! Cuckoo!

APOLLO.
Why bird? What song is this?

CROW.
I do not sing amiss – For all thy worthiness
For all thy beauty and thy gentillese
For all thy songs and minstrelsy
I sing thy wife doth cuckold thee!
If I sing false let me not thrive
Upon thy bed I saw her swyved –

APOLLO.
No!

CROW.
Cuckoo! I saw her swyved –

APOLLO.
No! No!

CROW.
They're at it now!

The MAN *makes a dash for it.* APOLLO *shoots his* WIFE *with a silver arrow then breaks his bow, arrows and all his musical instruments.*

APOLLO.
O dearest wife! Jewel of womanhood!
Alas! I was inflamed to do this deed.
O traitor crow!

CROW.
Who me! Cuckoo!

APOLLO.
Cursed be thy feathers! Cursed be thy tale
Though once thy song surpassed the nightingale
I shall in punishment bereft thy voice
Converting it to hideous noise!

CROW.
Caw! Caw! Caw!

APOLLO.
And thy white feathers – every one –
Henceforth be as black as Acheron!

He strikes the CROW *which turns black.*

CROW.
Caw! Caw! Caw!

MANCIPLE.
My mother warned me, when I was still young
To keep my council, and hold still my tongue:
'My son beware, and be not author new,
Of any tidings – be they false or true.
And when thou speakst, be it to high or low
Guard well thy tongue, and think upon the crow.'

CHORUS.
Think ere ye speak, be it to high or low,
Best hold thy tongue, and think upon the crow.

Music. The PILGRIMS *approach the shrine of St Thomas.*

Twenty-One: The Parson's Prayer

PARSON.

We must approach the blessed martyr with faith, and with true penitence in our hearts for our sins. And, if we ask it, we shall have the strength of God and the protection of His angels. Then shall we understand what the fruits of penitence are. And, according to the word of Jesus Christ, those fruits are the endless bliss of heaven – there, joy hath no contraries of woe nor of grievance – there, all harms of this present life are passed – there, is safe refuge from the pains of hell – there, is the blissful company that rejoice evermore in each other's joy – there, the body of man that was once foul, and dark is clearer than is the sun – there, the body that once was sick, frail, feeble, and mortal is immortal, and so strong and whole that nothing may injure it – there, is neither any hunger, nor thirst, nor cold, but every soul is replenished with the sight, and the perfect knowing of God. And we pilgrims – how may we enter into the joys of heaven, we that seek them? This blissful reign may be purchased by spiritual poverty, glory accomplished by humbleness, the abundance of joy by a hunger and thirsting for righteousness, rest by labour, and the life eternal through death and the mortification of sin. Amen.

ALL.

Amen!
Kyrie, eleison.
Christe, eleison.
Kyrie, eleison.

End of Part Four.